THE REMINISCENCES OF
Elda Elwood Logue

INTERVIEWED BY
Paul Stillwell

U.S. Naval Institute • Annapolis, Maryland

Copyright © 1999

Preface

Hundreds of thousands of individuals experienced hard times during the Depression that gripped the United States in the 1930s and then found salvation—in the form of steady work—in the Navy that won World War II. Ed Logue, as he's known to his friends, is a representative of those hundreds of thousands who served their country so well during the war. He enlisted before the war began and remained on active duty for several months afterward. His story helps illuminate the contributions of what television anchorman Tom Brokaw has celebrated as America's "greatest generation."

During a large part World War II, Mr. Logue was an electrician's mate on board the battleship New York (BB-34). Commissioned in 1914, she was one of the oldest ships in the fleet by the time he reported aboard in the summer of 1941. By the time he left her five years later, she had been a target for the world's most modern weapon, the atomic bomb. He was present when the weapon was tested against ships at Bikini Atoll in the Marshall Islands in the summer of 1946.

This memoir tells of the atmosphere on board ship in that wartime era: the generosity of shipmates who paid for Mr. Logue to go home on leave early in the war, the long hours on watch, living conditions for enlisted personnel, convoy duty in the North Atlantic, shore bombardment and kamikazes when the battleship's 14-inch guns supported the invasions of Iwo Jima and Okinawa in early 1945, liberty experiences, and the wonderful reception accorded American sailors who went ashore in Scotland in between convoy runs to the British Isles.

In other vignettes, Mr. Logue tells of boot camp training with a hard-bitten chief petty officer who turned young men from a variety of backgrounds into sailors; the generosity of Henry Ford in training machinist's mates at his factory in Dearborn, Michigan; the personalities of various skippers of the New York; an anecdote about an unsuccessful attempt to replace the battery in the captain's automobile; the enjoyment Mr. Logue and his bride had while living in New York City during the time he received training at the Brooklyn Navy Yard; and the camaraderie that develops among men serving together in a great warship.

Captain David Durbin, a Naval Reserve lawyer who works in western Missouri, nominated Mr. Logue, a friend of his, for inclusion in the oral history program. I happened to be in that state in late 1995 to bring a son home for Christmas vacation from college, and so Mr. Logue and I were able to get together. Captain Durbin made his office available as the site of the interview, which explains why this is one of the few Naval Institute oral histories conducted in a federal courthouse. Captain Durbin was also helpful in providing followup information as the history moved along from raw transcripts to the finished product. Mr. Logue's sons have provided assistance as well.

Lieutenant Commander George Van, a retired naval officer who generously donates his time to the Naval Institute's oral history program, did an excellent job of transcribing Mr. Logue's interview tapes. Ann Hassinger of the Institute's history division has made a significant contribution to the project through her diligence in the overall process of printing, proofreading, and overseeing the binding of the completed volume.

Paul Stillwell
Director, History Division
U.S. Naval Institute
June 1999

ELDA ELWOOD LOGUE

Birthplace:

Whittier, California, 19 August 1921

Education:

Attended first five years of school in Pomona, California.

Attended school in Bentley, Kansas, from 1931 to high school graduation in 1939.

Took accounting courses at Wichita Business College, Wichita, Kansas, following World War II.

Military Service:

Enlisted in the U.S. Navy, 3 December 1940

Recruit training at Great Lakes, Illinois

Machinist's mate school at Dearborn, Michigan

Assigned to the battleship New York (BB-34) in 1941.

- Immediately preceding World War II, the New York was active in the North Atlantic, enforcing U.S. neutrality.
- In July 1941 she escorted troopships to Reykjavik, Iceland, and also to Newfoundland.
- In 1942 the ship made convoy runs to Scotland, later supported the invasion of North Africa while Mr. Logue was attending a Navy school in New York.
- From July 1943 to June 1944, the New York trained personnel from the U.S. Navy, Coast Guard, and Allied navies while serving as a gunnery school in Chesapeake Bay. She also operated between Annapolis, Maryland, and Trinidad, British West Indies, while training Naval Academy midshipmen.
- On 21 November 1944 the New York went through the Panama Canal and then steamed to San Pedro, California. She underwent an extensive program of gunnery training.
- In early 1945 the ship proceeded to Pearl Harbor, Hawaii, and subsequently took part in the operations to capture the islands of Iwo Jima and Okinawa. She later returned to Pearl Harbor and was there when World War II ended in August 1945.

- Following the war, the ship made several trips back and forth to Pearl Harbor to bring troops back to the United States.
- Logue was head of the New York's electric shop in 1946 when the ship went to Bikini Atoll in the Marshall Islands for use in atomic bomb tests there.

Temporary duty in late 1946 on board the cruisers Pasadena (CL-65) and Columbus (CA-74)

Discharged from the U.S. Navy in January 1947 as electrician's mate first class.

Civilian Employment:

Grocery store in Bentley, Kansas, 1947-48

High school in Bentley, Kansas, 1948-49

Bareco Oil Company, Wichita, Kansas, 1949-53

Phillips Petroleum Company, Wichita, Kansas, 1953-73

Kansas Turnpike, Wichita, Kansas, 1973-86

Retired August 1986

Family:

Married the former Bertha May "Mickey" Maxwell on 14 October 1942

Son Larry Allen Logue, born 12 October 1947

Son Michael Edward Logue, born 11 October 1953

Authorization

The U.S. Naval Institute is hereby authorized to make available to individuals, libraries, and other repositories of its choosing the transcripts of an oral history interview concerning the life and naval service of the undersigned. The interview was recorded on 13 December 1995 in collaboration with Paul Stillwell for the U.S. Naval Institute.

The undersigned does hereby release and assign to the U.S. Naval Institute all right, title, restrictions, and interest in the interviews. The copyright in both the oral and transcribed versions shall be the sole property of the U.S. Naval Institute. The tape recordings of the interviews are and will remain the property of the U.S. Naval Institute.

Signed and sealed this _FIRST_ day of _JANUARY_ 1996.

E. E. Logue
E. E. Logue

Interview with Mr. Elda Elwood Logue

Place: Jackson County Courthouse, Kansas City, Missouri*

Date: Wednesday, 13 December 1995

Interviewer: Paul Stillwell

Paul Stillwell: If you would just say a few words for your voice level, please.

Mr. Logue: Well, I was talking about my uncle, Elda Myers, that came to live with us. He was my mother's half-brother. He was an old bachelor but a wonderful old man.

Paul Stillwell: Please tell me about your uncle.

Mr. Logue: All right. Well, we came down from Whittier, California. I was born in August of 1921, and I was the youngest. The family was formerly from Kansas, but at that time we were living in Whittier. My uncle was working up in Washington. My grandmother was still alive, and it's important that we remember that. She was still alive, but mother hadn't seen her half-brother for a good number of years, and there he was alone up there. So she wrote and invited him to come down and make his home with us, which he did. He was there, of course, when I was born, and I suppose that's one of the reasons that they named me for his first name. Now, I would have been glad to have had his second name--that was Eugene--instead of Elwood. But Elwood was a cousin of Dad's, and he had to get his in there, so that's the only reason that I can think of.

Paul Stillwell: And your uncle's first name was Elda?

Mr. Logue: Yes, Elda. E-L-D-A. Now, he was smart enough to put an H after his, and I should have done the same thing, but it wouldn't have been legal, I guess.

---

*Captain David S. Durbin, JAGC, USNR, recommended Mr. Logue for this oral history and generously made his courthouse office available as the site of the interview.

Paul Stillwell: What sort of work did your father do in California?

Mr. Logue: Anything he could get. My dad was a Kansas farmer, and that's really all he knew. He never got out of what they called the second reader, but my mother, who was a schoolteacher, helped teach him. He got to the point where he could read and do most anything anybody else would from an education point of view.

I'm not even quite sure why they came out to California, but they did. I think Mother wanted to come out. Grandma wanted them to come out--that was Mother's mother--and she financed part of it and so forth. But California at that time was strictly agriculture: nearly all orange groves and that sort of thing. You didn't see much business going on. But he worked in orange groves and even in some of the ranches out there and one thing and another, when he could work. It got pretty rough.

Paul Stillwell: Even in the '20s?

Mr. Logue: Yes. It got real rough there for a while, especially about the time that we left. And my uncle, bless his heart--oh, he was a worker, and very particular with his work. He loved flowers. Between him and my mother, who also loved flowers, they had a beautiful place around our place there in Pomona, California. That's where we moved before my memory, so the only thing I remember of living was there in Pomona.

He worked for the gas company in Pomona and, bless his heart, he supported us for two or three years there. My dad couldn't get any work at all to speak of. He worked six days a week in those days, and he made $25.00 a week, of which he turned $20.00 a week over to Dad every paycheck for our family--six kids, Mother and Dad and himself. Kept $5.00 for himself and that was all. Course, that was quite a bit of money in those days. That was enough to buy his tobacco and his cigars, and that was the main thing he wanted.

Paul Stillwell: Well, how did he support himself?

Mr. Logue: He lived with us.

Paul Stillwell: I see.

Mr. Logue: He had a room with us. Wherever we were at, he was part of our family--always was--right up to the day that--well, he outlived Mother and Dad both. Finally we had to put him in one of these senior citizen homes there in Wichita. But he had a nice place of his own. Of course, we had him out for Sunday quite often at our place and so on. So this went on till he finally passed away. But that's the story of the uncle. He was a wonderful old man. Oh, boy, he did love his pipe and his tobacco--oh, but he was probably one of the nicest, gentlest, friendliest, and most generous men that I ever knew in my life.

Paul Stillwell: Obviously generous to support your family.

Mr. Logue: As long as he did. But, of course, it worked the other way. When he was out of work, he was part of the family, and Dad supplied him with money for his tobacco and so on and so forth. So it was an easy go either way.

Paul Stillwell: Did you start school out there in California?

Mr. Logue: Yes, I did. I went to the first grade at Lincoln School in Pomona. They moved it up to Kauffman School later, but I was there through what we called in Pomona the low fifth. In 1932 it just got destitute around there, and Dad had about all he could stand. And it seemed that there was a farm in Missouri, just out of West Plains. It was a 90-acre farm, of which 50 acres was timber, 40 acres was under cultivation, and anything to get him some ground. And the people wanted Dad's place awfully bad. Well, there was a $400.00 mortgage on our house left yet to be paid. There was a $400.00 mortgage on that farm to be paid. And so they traded straight up and down, right straight across. So we loaded up everything we had.

By that time my two oldest sisters were married and in their own homes, and my oldest brother was married. So that left Loren and Paul, the two brothers just older than me, and then myself. Paul was seven years older than I was. I wasn't expected at all, I'm sure. But, in any event, Loren had an old Hupmobile touring car. We got a two-wheel trailer, and we loaded the back of that touring and loaded the trailer with everything they could to take. Then we took out in a 1926 Chevrolet sedan and that touring and headed for Missouri.

Paul Stillwell: Sort of like the Okies in reverse.*

Mr. Logue: Almost. Of course, the folks had friends along the way; I didn't know any of them. Finally we got down there. This is going to be a little better than you think before we finish. But we got down there and went out and found the place and oh, my gosh.

Paul Stillwell: So nobody in the family had seen it before.

Mr. Logue: That's right. Sight unseen, see. Oh, mercy. The house was horrible and the barn was worse. It was about to fall over. We went into the kitchen, and I'm telling you the truth. You could look up and what should have been a ceiling was boards up there, cracks between them, and you could see where they had hung tobacco in the kitchen to cure. Oh, boy, I'm telling you. We went back to town.

My mother was always in very poor health, at least in my memory. She had blood clots, she had a bad heart. From time to time she had dropsy that made her swell all up--several things like that that were really quite serious. When we got back, the strain was too much for her. So we got ahold of a Church of God--they were Church of God people, good Christian people--and they got ahold of a minister there in West Plains who found an empty house and got permission. We took springs and mattress in and laid mother on the temporary bed of that kind and tried to figure out what to do. By the way, too, I think Dad would have stayed and tried to make a go of that, but it was sold to him that the place was open; there was nobody on it. But when he got there, there was a renter on there with a crop out. Well, you can't put a man off if you've got a crop out, you know,

---

*During the great Depression of the 1930s, people from Oklahoma and elsewhere in the Midwest traveled to California in the hope of finding better job prospects there.

so there we were. So then when Mother got to feeling better, why, we came back over into Kansas. Now, Dad was a Kansas farmer.

Paul Stillwell: Was this still in 1932?

Mr. Logue: Yes, there was only a few days there at West Plains.

Paul Stillwell: I see.

Mr. Logue: We came back, and we stopped at Columbus, where we had friends. They had that awful sulfur water there. And that dear friend of Mother said, "Oh, you must stay here because this is healthy water. It might even cure you." So Dad rented a place there, and he couldn't get a job in Columbus, so he left and went back over around Bentley, Kansas. Now, that's where I grew up. That area. And, of course, he knew people there, so he got work on a farm. He would work a couple of weeks and come home and spend a week with us, and then he'd go back. Did that nearly all summer long. Well, it wasn't helping mother. The water certainly wasn't helping me. And Uncle Elda stayed there with us too.

So then in August, why, he found a place to rent--an old three-room house. By the time you give Uncle Elda one of them rooms, there weren't many rooms left for Dad and Mother and I. But we moved back into that little house, and we was only there, I think, a couple of months until he was able to rent a nice 160-acre farm. Nice house and everything on it. Of course, there were no improvements like electricity or anything like that in those days out in rural, but it was very nice. It had nice out buildings and so forth. He was able to take possession of it in February, the following year. So that's when life began. I learned how to farm under my Dad, and we farmed that until 1939.

Paul Stillwell: What sort of crops?

Mr. Logue: Corn, and that's where he made one of his big mistakes. Those from 1932 or '33 up through 1938 were the driest, hottest years Kansas has ever known. If he'd have put wheat out--well, the only times he did it was just a bad luck run. He had one crop of wheat that he was able to harvest. That's when they put the binders in the field and brought the threshing machine in for threshing crews. A year or so later, he thought he'd try to make it again because his corn burned up every year.

So he put out the wheat, and I think he had a good 80-acre patch of the most beautiful wheat you ever saw in your life. He was going to make it--finally, at last. And, of course, combines were just coming out then, and they talked him into leaving it for the combine; they could get it all at once. And would you believe, the night before the combine got there, a wind and rain storm come and laid that wheat flat to the ground and in those days they didn't have anything to pick it up with. Sam Stanback had the combine. He made one round, come back, and he said, "Arthur, I can't even cut enough wheat to pay for your cutting."

He said, "I can't help it. I've got to give the landlord a third of the wheat."

"Why," he said, "I'll talk to your landlord." So he did, and they told him to forget it, and that was the wheat crop. So he had the roughest luck. He had a fellow that backed him on the farm, a good friend of his, an old cattleman that had come over from England with his family years and years before. He just seemed to think the world of Dad and all of us. He was the kindest old fellow. He lent Dad the money and everything. Well, at the time he went off the farm, my Dad owed him $237.00, which was still quite a bit of money back then.

Paul Stillwell: Plus you still owed $400.00 on that place in West Plains.

Mr. Logue: Oh, that West Plains. There's a funny story to that. When it came due, I think in about 1936 maybe or 1935, somewhere along in there, he just let it go back. It wasn't worth $400.00 to him. Dad had a friend, a fellow by the name of Lawrence Owens, a big old fellow--he never did a day's work in his life, but he was a wheeler and dealer if you ever heard one. He came over there and, of course, I was just a kid and I loved to sit around and listen to those guys talking. Lawrence came over there, and he said, "Arthur, what are you going to do with that farm over there in West Plains?"

He said, "Funny you should ask. The mortgage is going to take it next week." He said, "I'm going to let them have it."

"Oh, you can't do that. Not a farm like that."

"Oh, yeah," he said. "I can't come up with the money, and I don't want the place."

"Oh, it's got to be worth more than the $400.00, my word." He said, "Why don't you sell it to me?"

"Well," he says, "you can have it." So they went down to the bank and the notary, and in those days you had to pay a dollar. So he had to pay Dad a dollar, and they signed the paperwork and got a go. Two weeks later he come back and wanted his dollar back. [Laughter] So that's what happened to the farm. [Laughter] Well, anyhow, we finished up there, and he left owing $237.00.

Dad wasn't in very good health, either, but he went out, and he shucked corn and worked and did everything he could. I have and treasure that check, $237.00, that he worked and paid off that mortgage.

Paul Stillwell: So he was a hired hand from then on.

Mr. Logue: From then on until he completely--well, I think along about--see, he passed away in '45, so he would have got in on the old age pension or whatever it was there for a while, and he remarried. My mother died in '35. She was 56. But her health had been real bad. Now, we stayed on the farm until the end of 1938, first of '39. Then we moved to town, and then I graduated from high school that year.

Paul Stillwell: This was in Columbus?

Mr. Logue: No, no, this was Bentley, Kansas. I didn't tell you about the move up from Columbus in August. I think I did mention that we moved up to Bentley and got that three-room house and moved over to the farm. And then from the farm we moved to a house in town, and Dad remarried and he went to live in her house. I graduated from high school then and went out on my own.

Paul Stillwell: Please tell me about your schooling in Kansas.

Mr. Logue: Well, I went through grade school in Kansas. I had gone to and finished the last part of the fifth grade in Columbus. Then I came back to the sixth grade, and in Bentley you had three grades in there: fourth, fifth and sixth. Then the high school building was a different building entirely, and they were kind of short on students in their school. They had an extra room so that--now, they had two different boards of education. We got the grade school board of education and the high school board of education there at that time. So they got together and worked out a deal, and they were able to move the seventh and eighth grades to this one room in the high school building. And we were still under the auspices of the grade school organization, but we used that room and had the one teacher for both grades, so I had my seventh and eighth grade in that room. And then after I graduated from the eighth grade, I went on to high school in the same building and finished high school there in Bentley.

Paul Stillwell: Would you have any comparison of the quality of the education in California and in Kansas?

Mr. Logue: Well, I don't think it was that much difference, at least in my life. I had good teachers in Kansas, and I had good teachers in California.

Paul Stillwell: So it was no problem making an adjustment.

Mr. Logue: Not at all. Not for me at least, and we got by very well. I never was a real whoopee student. I was always wanting to have too much fun, but then I got by. I wasn't an A student, but I wasn't a flunker either. [Chuckle]

Paul Stillwell: What subjects were particularly interesting to you?

Mr. Logue: I was interested in, actually, science and history. Those two were my favorites. And, of course, we didn't have any such thing as trade areas to explore or anything like that in those days. But I did. I enjoyed those two more. I did not particularly like English. I'm ashamed of myself, but I didn't like the breaking down of the sentences and all that stuff. And I wasn't really too fond of literature. I read a lot of it, but it left me a little cold, English literature and so forth. But I made it. I didn't flunk any of them, but I didn't make any great raves either in my grades.

Paul Stillwell: Did you pick up mechanical skills on the farm?

Mr. Logue: Yes.

Paul Stillwell: What sorts of things?

Mr. Logue: Well, we had to farm with animals--with mules--and we had to make our own repairs on our equipment. But our equipment was very simple. We had cultivators, one team on a cultivator with wheels and a seat behind--you've possibly seen them. And that's how we cultivated our corn. I told you he raised corn most of the time. That's all he ever did years before, and I think about one year he got a fair crop. But most of the time, I know we'd go out in the field--now, talk about making your own--Dad was the maker and the mechanic. He took 2 by 4s, made two of them I'm going to say, oh, about 6, 7 feet long--kind of cut them on the ends so they could be used as runners. And then he got one back here maybe four feet. And he got a--do you know what a stock cutter is?

Paul Stillwell: No.

Mr. Logue: All right. This is a machine that has blades that rotate, that're hooked to the wheels. And you can disconnect them from the wheels or let them go. They will come down and when you go through a field that you've already shucked the corn on and you want to chop that corn up, get ready so you can plow your ground, you drop that down and it comes around like that and cuts the furrow. You've got, oh, four to six blades. Now, that blade's about that long, about that thick, and it's kept reasonably sharp.

So the reason I wanted you to understand that is because we take a blade off that stock cutter--Dad did--and he bolted it on this particular platform that he built at an angle. He put an apple box on there, and on that apple box he put me. And he got a mule out here in the front. I went down the rows of that corn which didn't produce any ears, and I would catch it like this against that knife and get an armload and carry it over and put it on the pile. Later we took it in and put it around the corral, and that's what we fed the animals in the winter time. That's all we could come up with.

Things like that you made your own. You just made what you needed, and that's what you did. Does that answer your question on that? There wasn't a great deal of things--my brother Loren was a mechanic. I'd like to say, if I can, about him that he was remarkable in some ways and very foolish in others. He didn't care about a career for himself. He didn't care for a lot of money or anything like that, but he loved the things that he did.

But to me one of the most outstanding was that we had a neighbor who was down the road and across the road. He had about 40 acres of corn. This guy had money, and he had faith in Loren. So they did something Kansas had never had and a lot of other states. They put down a well. He took a 6-inch pipe--I'm going to say about 10 feet long--and he took a cutting torch and he cut lengths about 6 inches long, staggered all the way around. They wrapped it with coarse screen and then with hail screen on the outside. And they buried that, so you could go down and catch water anywhere from 12 to 20 feet there, all you wanted, in that part of the country. So they sunk that as a point to a well, if you're following me. Okay.

The pipe on top of that they welded it and brought it on up. They got an old pump that had been used in a sand pit and hooked on to that, and then they got us out there in front with a board over the discharge end and put that monkey goo around it there so that you could pump it with a pitcher pump, if you believe. We primed that thing. I think it took a day and a half to do it. But we finally got it finished. As quick as the water came out, I mean they hit her--the engine was ready--shot the water out of there.

Well, that's how it started. And they got that thing and made an irrigating well out of it. That year he irrigated that 40 acres. He bought some canvas hose--I think about 8 or 9 inches in diameter. We spread that out, and we just kept moving it around. We had three shifts. I worked the night shift. The next year then he modified it and did a lot better. Now, the point I'm trying to make is that that's the first irrigation that had ever been known in that part of the country. And I remember in my evening shift guys come up from Oklahoma, they come from Nebraska, from Missouri--everywhere--to see that irrigating.

I went to the Navy. Six years later I come back, and you saw an irrigating plant on pretty near every farm. And it started with old uncle Loren. So I was kind of proud of him. But he could build anything he wanted to, and he made a pump one time. He took a gas pipe--I want to call it--or it would be a water pipe because it was more like an inch and a half in diameter--and he made a little propeller, and he took a welding rod and welded that on the bottom of it. He made some little things like bearings on the inside that would support that shaft going up and down. He put a little pulley on the top of it. And he got a belt off a sewing machine and he backed off a six-volt battery and a little six-volt electric motor.

Said, "Now, you hold that pipe." I was just a kid now, and he said, "When you hold that pipe, you put it down into that water, in that bucket there that I have."

"Okay."

"All right, put her down in there." Pretty near drowned me. [Laughter] Just things like that. Yet he could do anything to a car. He could repair it anytime. Kept all of our cars running and all. So that pretty well describes the mechanics. It was all with him. I never was a mechanic to any great store or anything like that.

Paul Stillwell: Sounds like there was no room in your life for luxuries at that point.

Mr. Logue: Not a bit. Not a bit. No, sir.

Paul Stillwell: Did you have a radio?

Mr. Logue: No. No, we didn't have a radio till we went to town, and then we had a little bitty old one that we plugged in. Now, Paul, you were wondering about what got me interested in the Navy, I think. Are you ready for that? Let's see.

[Interruption]

Paul Stillwell: We were talking about the fact that you didn't have any luxuries.

Mr. Logue: No, that's true. Just the radio.

Paul Stillwell: Probably no movies.

Mr. Logue: Well, we had little theaters in the smaller towns around. There was, you know, nothing in our town. Don't know whether you're interested in how I met the wife or not.

Paul Stillwell: Well, sure.

Mr. Logue: I never had time or money, and I was also very bashful. So I never had much of a dating program. Once or twice maybe--and that was about it--coming through high school.

Now, my cousin was about my age. Her father died before she was born. He was the younger brother of my dad's. Her mother married again, and that's kind of a messed-up deal. She married into a large family of kids, and they just kind of ordered Florence around as a servant about all the time. She finally came and lived with us, I know, one winter, to kind of get out of it. Mother took to her right away and was very good to her, and she loved Dad. Dad was the nearest thing to a dad that she had, was old Art. And Dad was awful good to her. So she came, and we got to be real good friends.

Maybe two or three years later, something like that, I'd just started to shave. Dad had a mirror that hung right there on the west wall of the kitchen, so that in the evening sun came in and gave him light. He was like me; he had bad eyes. I just wonder to this day if it was cataracts, which is what it turned out to be on me. Anyhow, that way he could see, and all we had was an old straight-edge razor and razor strop. So I was learning to shave, and here come Florence in the car with another girl with her. And, I tell you, there I was, half-shaven. I saw the prettiest girl I ever saw in my life.

Paul Stillwell: What year was this?

Mr. Logue: Nineteen thirty-seven--maybe toward the end of it or something like that. And she just came over there, and this girl came in with her and introduced me and, man, she was a sweetheart. And so friendly and nice and just a warm person. I mean, I fell right then. But she was a little older than I was--about two years older--and, of course, that makes a difference when you're only 16. And I couldn't get that girl off my mind. I never did.

So then, a year and a half or so later when I graduated from high school, we were living in town at that time, and my oldest brother and his family came out. He took a vacation, and he come out for his little brother's graduation and visit too. Florence had never met him. That would be her cousin. And, of course, she was interested. So she come a-roaring over there one Saturday afternoon, and we was all around there, and she met him. Finally she got me aside and says, "You're going to have to get me a date."

Well, that was ridiculous. That gal was hot number one. She was ready. I mean, nice girl and all that, but then everybody was wanting to date Florence. She was a good-looking girl and a lot of fun. I said, "What do you mean, get you a date? When did you ever need any help getting dates?"

She said, "Well, I got you one."

I said, "That's worse then ever. Who have you got?"

She said, "Mickey."[*]

I said, "Who do you want?" [Laughter] That was it. That was the girl.

So I called a guy I knew by the name of Orie Reed that had always been wanting to go with Florence. And, boy, he was up and ready, so he and I went over and picked the girls up that night in Mount Hope, and that was the first date on a Saturday night. And I never missed a Saturday night after that. I had her dated up every Saturday night. [Laughter] Well, it just went on from there, and when I saw I wasn't going to be able to get--I worked for farmers that summer. There was nothing to do, I wasn't trained for anything.

My brother, this Loren that I told you was a mechanic, was writing me from California. He was out there. "Oh, if you come out here, you can get a job easy." So they

---

[*]Mickey was the nickname of Mr. Logue's future wife, Bertha Mae Maxwell.

used to have those little buses; $10.00 or $15.00, you could get on in Wichita and a whole bunch of people ride with a guy, and he'd buy him a new car and he'd pay for it that way. They were illegal, but then they did it.

So I took one of them out there. It cost me $15.00. Couldn't find a thing. I think I helped fertilize an orange grove one time walking up and down and throwing the stuff out around the trees. Couldn't get any work anywhere. So I stayed out there two or three months. "Oh, wait till spring, wait till we get into it," he said. I was staying with him in his little cabin there. Never did any good, so I came back.

My brother-in-law was pretty much up the construction company with Mitry Brothers Construction. He was master mechanic there for them. He was sharp as a tack. And he got me a job. They were building a dam down there just out of Cherokee, Oklahoma, on the Salt Fork River, and he got me a job, pick and shovel. Well, that was all right. I was used to that. In those days, all we knew was work. And they didn't have the scoops and stuff they've got nowadays. They just had crews with pick and shovel. So we were out there digging weep holes on the side of the dam, and I think they put about six or eight guys to what they called a straw boss. And all he did was stand back there and watch you.

They assigned you a pick and assigned you a shovel--checked them out to you, and they were your responsibility. And so you went out, and you would dig. They showed you what to dig, so you kept that pick a-going, and let me tell you. You stop and lean on that and start visiting, that straw boss is right there. He's taking a look at you, and he'd grab that thing and [noise of a struggle], like that, you know, hand it back to you. He was trying to intent what he expected, so you got at it again. And the second time if he had to do it, you went down the road. They had people lined up for that job.

Paul Stillwell: What was the pay for this job?

Mr. Logue: Forty-five cents an hour. I worked six days a week, which was a blessing. And I was making money at that time. So I worked there then all summer. That was just before I went to the Navy, and by the time I went to the Navy I was in good shape.

Paul Stillwell: I'll bet you were.

Mr. Logue: I kid you not. And I was overweight. I can't remember how much. Shall we go on from there now?

Paul Stillwell: I have just one more question about the '30s. How much were you able to keep up with current events, such as the things over in Europe with the dictators and so forth?

Mr. Logue: I think pretty much by newspaper. Well, a lot of people had radios, and, like I said, we had that one in town. But we always took a newspaper, and that kept us pretty well--

The thing that you need to remember, and lots of people don't, is that when us guys went into the Navy, we knew nothing about war. Today everybody knows about war. There's been nothing but war since World War II. But back then there had been no war since World War I. All we knew was some of the stories or maybe some of the movies they made or something like that about what went on. So let me tell you, it made a difference; it made a difference.

Paul Stillwell: Did you have any understanding with Mickey when you were going away to the Navy, or had you already married?

Mr. Logue: Yes, we did. Yes, we did. We had decided to get married, and we had decided to wait until six years was up and get married after I got out. That way she wouldn't be caught with children if anything happened to me, and so on. We were afraid maybe that--

Paul Stillwell: That's a patient woman.

Mr. Logue: Yes. Well, it was her idea.

Paul Stillwell: I see.

Mr. Logue: Yes, it was her idea. I would have gone sooner. But we did. I'll tell you more about that.

Paul Stillwell: Okay.

Mr. Logue: What caused me to want to go to the Navy was my brother Paul went to the Navy in 1935 and came out then four years later in '39. He got into the machinist's mate department of it and came out and got some good jobs working at power plants and one thing and another. He was in the steam part of it, you know, their boilers and so on and so forth, because of his experience. And he had a pretty good line the rest of his life.

Paul Stillwell: Did he serve in ships?

Mr. Logue: Yes, for most of his time, he was on the USS <u>Pensacola</u>, a heavy cruiser.

Paul Stillwell: So some of this sort of rubbed off on you.

Mr. Logue: Well, in this way. The Army--oh, pretty good uniforms. You know, as a kid you think about that--and Marines. I was getting close to the Marines, but, then again, I wanted a trade. And I knew that there was a trade there in the Navy, and that's what I decided. What really tipped me over was trying to get in there and learn a trade.

    I didn't really want to join up for six years. I will have to say this part of my life because I think it has a bearing. Always had a good ear for music, thank the Lord, and my Dad was good. He was a whale of an old-time fiddler. He was very good. I learned to play the guitar, and we played for a lot of square dances around over the country and things like that and used to sing a lot and so forth.

    Before I went, why, they had a group known as the Ark Valley Boys on the radio there at KFH in Wichita. That was the main big station in Wichita in those days. I noticed they were up short a man one time from their trio and after two or three days--they would come on during the noon hour--that was part of their time for everyday, and then they also had outside jobs and so forth. So I thought, "Well, that guy--he's missing for some reason."

Mickey and I were going together, and she went with me and I went down and called up and asked if I could come down and try out. They said, "Sure, come on down." So I did, and we went into the auditorium on rehearsal night. Then they called me up and gave me a guitar and asked me to sing them a song, so I did. Well that impressed them. They liked that. So they put me in.

Well, I'll tell you something I learned. I loved singing, and I loved quartet, I loved harmony and I could hear it, but you know, the third part, if you're familiar with it at all--we call it the baritone--the third part on a quartet or something like that--it's usually between bass and lead, and the tenor's on top. It's not the easiest part to hear, and not very many people sing it. So I thought, "Ah ha, now that's the thing. If I can learn to pick up that third part with my ear, then I'll have a lot better chance to get into quartets and all than I would, because there's tenors and basses all over the place."

So I'd turn on that radio. Every time I could find a duet, I'd get up there and listen to them. With my ear I'd pick out the harmony part that would go with them and sing along with them, you know. Well, in time you take to where you can adjust yourself to how you're going to be able to stay with them. So I got up, and I could sing the third part with them. And the guys that were there were impressed.

I'd also play the fiddle for them a little. Well, I was nothing like Dad, and I didn't make any big impression. The guy that owned the thing, I guess, came in about that time from Nebraska, and they was telling him all about me. He listened to me sing one time, says, "We'll let you know." And that was it. Well, shoot. I went down to the recruiting station. Well, let's go back now. I went to the recruiting station long before that. I went to the recruiting station about the last of September.

Paul Stillwell: What year was this now?

Mr. Logue: This was 1940, and the Navy wasn't looking for people. Now, the Army was. The Army was already drafting 21-year-olds. But the Navy wasn't interested at all at that time. And the Navy recruiter in Wichita said, "Well, we don't have a draft going here, but when we get one I'll put your name down and give you a call."[*]

This would have been then right around the last part of November, because I didn't get my call till about the second of December of 1940. A couple of other guys that I went to school with got on the list, too, somehow or another, so the three of us went together. There I was--always overweight, you know--and I thought, "Well, we'll go up there." They called us. We got on the train and went up to Kansas City. That's where they give us our first big go-around. I figured they were going to wash me out and take those guys, but it was just the other way around. Sent those two lugs home and took me.

Paul Stillwell: Why?

Mr. Logue: Well, one of them had jock itch, and they told him to go back and straighten it up. And the other one had a little problem with his lungs or something. It wasn't anything serious; they just weren't taking them. So I went on back to Great Lakes, and, of course, you know what they did.[†] They took all my clothes away and put them in a box and sent them home. Walked around from one room to another without any clothes. We go in there and we get our physical.

Paul Stillwell: And this was in December?

Mr. Logue: Actually, this was the third day of December--we're over to the third day. And I'd already signed up. I mean, they'd already taken me but then on their terms, not mine.

Paul Stillwell: What would your terms have been? Would they have been any different from the Navy's terms?

---

[*] In this context, "draft" refers to a group of men traveling together from the recruiting station to the site of their induction or initial naval training. It differs from "draft" used in the earlier sentence, which refers to taking men into the Army through conscription.
[†] Recruit training, known more commonly as boot camp, was conducted at the Naval Training Station, Great Lakes, Illinois, about 30 miles north of downtown Chicago on the shore of Lake Michigan.

Mr. Logue: Not really. One thing that I grew up with was that I learned discipline a long time ago in our home. And not cruel. Dad was never cruel, but he was stern and firm. So I didn't have the trouble with discipline that a lot of guys that came in did. I was used to it and willing to accept it. Oh, you get ruffled, of course, I mean, at times, but that wasn't a big thing with me.

Paul Stillwell: Did you have any problems with homesickness? That's a common one too.

Mr. Logue: Yes. Yes. Sure, I did. Not serious, but several times before it was over with, you sure wondered what in the world you was doing in that place.

Paul Stillwell: Well, but frequently they keep you so busy you don't have time to think about that.

Mr. Logue: This is true, but then there was always night time.

Paul Stillwell: That's true.

Mr. Logue: Especially when you're trying to hang on and stay in your hammock.

Paul Stillwell: Well, please tell me about boot camp.

Mr. Logue: Well, we were given our clothes, of course, and you know how that happened. Then we went over to our barracks, and here come this old chief boatswain's mate, and he looked like he was about 70 years old. He was our trainer, and we learned to march first and then we got our rifles. We went through all that good stuff and everything. I think the main thing that stands out in my mind on boot camp was the hammocks.

Paul Stillwell: Well, please tell me about those.

Mr. Logue: Well, you know what they were, don't you? You saw them.

Paul Stillwell: I want to hear it in your words.

Mr. Logue: All right. They put those things up and strung them tight, and they insisted you have to sleep on them tight, or you'd ruin your kidneys. And so it was an experience to try to get in, especially for the first time. You were--bump--right over on the deck. And you come back, and you try it again and you grab this. Finally, you get in, and you're just laying there like this and the guy comes up beside you--well, what's he going to do?--he grabs for you to steady him--whomp, you both go over. And this just went on for a while. I don't think we got any sleep for a week.

Paul Stillwell: The deck is hard.

Mr. Logue: Yes, it is. And you're lucky to land on your feet. [Laughter] So we fought that. We fought them probably, I think, for a good week before we could get much sleep. And then get out and drill every day, but eventually, like anything else, you learn. Shoot, I got eventually where I could learn to relax in that thing, turn over, anything I wanted to do. Sounds crazy, but it's just a matter of tuning yourself to it, I guess.

Paul Stillwell: Much like riding a bicycle.

Mr. Logue: There you are. Exactly. So that was the thing that stood out as much as anything. There was another thing. I think about the second day we were there some kid had enough of it and he run up on the radio tower and jumped off. Oh, that didn't do our morale any good. But, of course, we're young, and we're not used to stuff like that. I mean, myself, and all. The old man was pretty good to us. He was rough, and it was important for him to be, looking back on it. I wouldn't change a thing.

Paul Stillwell: Did you get the sense that he was trying to weed out people that couldn't make it?

Mr. Logue: I never really thought of it in that point of view. Maybe it was, because I was too young and too busy with my own problems. I never really stood back and looked at it from the outside.

Paul Stillwell: Did you lose some of the people from your group?

Mr. Logue: Don't think we did. If we did, I can't remember it. I think the old man was just determined to make a sailor out of every one of us, and he took the time to do it. And he didn't do it in a brotherly fashion either. [Laughter] He came down on us, but I think it was probably the best thing he could do. Right away, we learned what was expected of us in the Navy.

Paul Stillwell: Do you remember a spirit of camaraderie developing with the other men in your group?

Mr. Logue: Oh, yes. Yes, indeed. Now, I know you were in the Navy too.* I realized that when you talked about your chief, and I wondered if this ever struck you this way. But when I went in, there was tremendous competition and even beyond that, between the Navy, the Army, the Marines, and the Coast Guard and all that work.

Okay, break it down then to the ships. There was competition between those ships, and I don't mean just competition. It got pretty serious. Now, let's get down to the ship. The deck force and the engineers hardly have anything to do with each other, except when they were against another ship. Get down into the engineering force. Take the B division, take the A division, take the E division, take all of them. Just as much competition between every one of them. Now, we get down to the E division, where I spent most of my time. You've got the light shop, you've got the power shop, you've got the IC room, you've got the distribution--and we were all just as competitive--I mean, in there, we were for our own.

Now, from that, as you branch on out then, of course, there's your rates. I mean,

---
*The interviewer went through recruit training at Great Lakes, Illinois, in 1962.

you've got your first class and you're down to your striker.* [Laughter]

Paul Stillwell: Did you see that kind of competition in boot camp, between companies?

Mr. Logue: Oh, yes. Oh, absolutely. You bet. Yes, indeed. Everybody was trying to do their best; they really were. We were scared--I was, anyhow--a good deal of the time. I was scared because I didn't know for sure what was expected of me, and I'd always been taught to do what was right. I had to overcome it in time, but I don't know that I ever did. I always had a little bit of fear that, "Am I doing this thing right now and what can I do to get to where I can do it right?" Just kind of part of my nature, I guess, but it didn't overwhelm any part of me. I mean, I don't want you to think it was a major part of my thinking, but there was always that little bit of fear in there. Just stayed with me. Probably still there. I don't know.

Paul Stillwell: Well, I remember the same thing, because our chief would issue threats: "If you don't do so and so, we'll kick you out, and then you'll get drafted into the Army."

Mr. Logue: He didn't do that. He said, "You run around that parade field for about 15 times." That's what he threatened us with, and after working all day that didn't sound very good. No, I never did hear a threat like that, really didn't. I think his name was Hepker, if I'm not mistaken. But, you know, we got pretty fond of that old man, and we all chipped in and bought him a present when we left, after the graduation. He broke down and cried. [Laughter]

Paul Stillwell: Do you remember course work, like learning The Bluejackets' Manual and that sort of thing?†

---

*A striker is a non-rated man who is in training for potential advancement to petty officer in a particular rating.
†The Bluejackets' Manual, which has been published by the U.S. Naval Institute in various editions over the years, has long been considered the "bible" for Navy enlisted men. It is a basic textbook and reference volume on a wide variety of naval subjects. Formerly these topics were addressed in chapters designated by letters from A to N.

Mr. Logue: Yes. You had that and you had to pass it or you couldn't graduate when it came time. But what was it? How long was detention? Do you remember? I was trying to think. I think it was a month.

Paul Stillwell: I don't know.

Mr. Logue: I think we were in there a month in detention, and then we went over to the other side, which they called Camp Paradise in Great Lakes. It was a long ways from paradise, but compared to detention it wasn't bad. [Laughter] Then they moved our hammocks up to where they were probably--oh, I would say--around five to six feet off the floor, to where you had to take a ladder to get into them.

Paul Stillwell: How high had they been initially?

Mr. Logue: Oh, about three feet.

Paul Stillwell: So you didn't have to fall so far.

Mr. Logue: This is true. We'd have broke all our necks if they hadn't. But we got to where we handled them real well. Well, over in Paradise we finished off. And then, like I said, I don't know. I never did think I was all that brilliant in school, but what was it, six? I think the top six they gave the choice of a trade school, and I got into that top six. I don't know how, but I did.

Paul Stillwell: Out of how many?

Mr. Logue: Well, 120-some guys in our company. So when I saw that there was a machinist school, why, right off the bat, I decided I wanted that. And then, when I found out we were going to Dearborn, that was better yet. So then, after we graduated--

Paul Stillwell: Well, before you graduate could you tell me about the effect of training in that cold weather?

Mr. Logue: Oh, that was rough. It was. But, yet, somehow, I don't have any bad memories of that. I'm sure I got cold and all of that, but I think I was so wrapped up in what was involved it kept me busy, my concentration on stuff like that, that I don't--I remember being awful cold, sure. But we had warm clothes. I have to put that in, all right.

Paul Stillwell: But you got used to that, along with everything else you were getting into.

Mr. Logue: I think so, because I have no bad memories--other than just you would, because we had that kind of weather at home in the winter time, and so I don't think that particularly bothered me.

Paul Stillwell: Well, they were feeding you regularly. Was the boot camp chow good?

Mr. Logue: No. No, I can definitely say I don't have the best memories for their chow, but then we didn't really eat like kings at home, either. [Laughter] So, again, I think, probably it was easier for me to adapt, looking back, than it might have been for some of the kids because, like I said, I was taught discipline and I had a loving father. I wouldn't want you to think he was mean or cruel in any way. But he required his boys to be what he expected them to be, and we learned that. We could have good fun with him, and, by the same token, you better do what in the world is right or you're going to get it. So I didn't have as much adapting over in some of that area as I might have had maybe coming from a different family. I don't know.

Paul Stillwell: Well, you had learned to make do with what you had.

Mr. Logue: This is it, and then, also, we didn't have big fancy meals either. Lots of times things were pretty scarce on the table. So, again, I don't have a bad memory of the food, other than I think it was more the idea that everybody thought it out to be, so we just said it was. On the long haul I don't think it was all that bad, really.

Paul Stillwell: Did they serve you beans and cornbread for breakfast?

Mr. Logue: Yes, they did. They sure did. That was one morning of the week that we got that. Probably the best breakfast there that they had. I didn't like their eggs for breakfast and I didn't like the unh-unh-unh on the shingle so much.* [Laughter] But outside of that--oh, we ate it, but, you know, it wasn't favored.

Paul Stillwell: Did you get liberty from boot camp?

Mr. Logue: Only after detention, but I never took it. I didn't know anybody, and the closest thing we had was that little town up north there.

Paul Stillwell: Waukegan?

Mr. Logue: Waukegan. And I just saved my money for boot leave, is what I did. We got about 13, 14 days of boot leave.

Paul Stillwell: What do you remember about inspections and taking care of your uniform?

Mr. Logue: Well, we learned the hard way. We learned with fear and trembling, and that's the truth. Because I've seen more than one guy--now, not so much with our old chief but if anybody from the bigger shots from the outside--we're still talking about chiefs--if he didn't like the looks of your bag when you had it laid out, he'd just pick it up and throw it at you--the whole thing, you know. You'd have to go out and wash it all over again, dry it and everything. It never happened to me, but I've seen it happen to a few of them. And, of course, that puts the fear in you.

---

*In this case, Mr. Logue's good manners kept him from saying "shit on a shingle," the slang term for creamed chipped beef on toast--also known as SOS.

But, as far as inspections, it wasn't anything I particularly enjoyed because I wasn't normally a neat person. [Laughter] I always worried about it, but then it wasn't an outstanding thing, you know, that was going to hurt my life or anything like that, I guess.

Paul Stillwell: Do you remember the drilling with rifles and so forth?

Mr. Logue: Yes. I got by with that pretty good. I never had a gun of my own. Well, we had an old shotgun there on the place and shot rabbits once in a while, but it wasn't a difficult thing for me learn, apparently, because I don't have bad memories of it at all. Some of them got pretty awkward, and they really got it all the time. I felt sorry for them but, no, I never did get called down. I got by pretty good with it.

Paul Stillwell: Part of boot camp is designed to build teamwork, so that you're working with the guy on either side of you and front and back.

Mr. Logue: You put it well. You put it well. That's true. I'd like to have said that myself, really, because I was anxious be part of the team in that. I think most of the guys were, and we all got along pretty good. I don't remember much problems in this course. We'd come in pretty tired at night and all that, but we were all pretty much companionable with one another.

Paul Stillwell: How did you spend your off time? Did you have any leisure hours?

Mr. Logue: Yes. Usually, you had a buddy, and you'd walk around the place, you know. In detention you'd walk down along the fence and watch the cars go by and tell each other stories and lies and one thing and another. [Laughter] You know, there'd be a companionship with some of the guys there mainly. That was about all you had. Then when we were in Paradise, why, there was a little more to do. They had some gyms, I think, and some stuff like that you could go to and all.

Paul Stillwell: Were you writing letters home during this whole period?

Mr. Logue: Oh, yes. I kept the letters going home to Dad and to Mickey.

After the graduation, like I said, we all chipped in and got the old man a present. I don't remember what it was now. And the old boy had tears in his eyes. But he bragged on us, "You were a good group--best group I ever had. I'd like to go to sea with you. I really would. I'd like to ship with you." Course, I don't know, but then it sounded good anyhow.

Paul Stillwell: Did you have a feeling of patriotism during that?

Mr. Logue: Yes, I did. I sure did. And I think we all did. Because we knew we were getting close to war. We weren't in it, but we knew that we weren't there just to play jacks.[*] I definitely felt that way, and I think most everyone did. Once in a while, you'd get some crackerjack, but then most of us felt that we had a pretty fine country. By George, we were proud of it, and we wanted to do the best we could for it. Maybe that sounds crazy, and I might not act like it all the time, but I really felt that way.

Paul Stillwell: Well, since it was voluntary, the people who were there probably were there because they wanted to be.

Mr. Logue: There you are. I think you're right there too. After boot leave--could I come back to that now?

Paul Stillwell: Sure.

Mr. Logue: I started in my school. Henry Ford II, who was a grandson, was an officer in the Navy.[†] He had nothing to do with that school, but I saw him off and on there in that Great Lakes area. I, of course never met him. But we had classroom for a month, and then they put us on a train to Dearborn.

---

[*]World War II had started in Europe in September 1939, which was 15 months before Mr. Logue enlisted.
[†]Ensign Henry Ford II, USNR, was the grandson of the famous inventor and automaker for whom he was named. In later life he served for many years as chairman of the Ford Motor Company.

Paul Stillwell: Where was the classroom work?

Mr. Logue: Are you familiar with Great Lakes?

Paul Stillwell: Vaguely.

Mr. Logue: Well, if you can remember where the barracks were for the--now I can't remember my directions--but this was a unit all by itself over there away from the rest of the buildings--the classrooms were--and they had offices and one thing and it was a one-story building.

They were enlisted men that were our teachers. They had given us a start out of the manual--our textbook--and we took tests on it and all. Once in a while an officer would come in and give us a lecture or something like that. But it was school. There was no horsing around. You either studied and tried, or out you went.

Paul Stillwell: Was this the rate training manual for machinist's mate?

Mr. Logue: Yes, I believe it was. Now, it's been a lot of years, but there was a manual. I think we had to turn it in for that class. And we made some notebooks up, I think, when we got to Dearborn. That's what I kept.

Paul Stillwell: How demanding was this course of study?

Mr. Logue: Well, at Great Lakes not so much. At Dearborn more so. Henry wasn't a man to fool around.* He was doing something great for the Navy. It wasn't costing the Navy one red dime. He built those barracks for the Navy. This might be a good enough place to tell you about meeting Henry Ford.

---

*Automaker Henry Ford operated this school at Dearborn, Michigan, for the benefit of the Navy. It was an adjunct to the Ford Motor Company.

Paul Stillwell: Sure.

Mr. Logue: Because he had a yacht, they told us, that he really liked. I mean, it was one of his favorites. Well, finally it just got so old they pulled it in and then dragged it out. He had them take all of the machinery part of it, that is the boiler, the dynamos and all that--water clearing and so forth--and put it in a building. Now, this was the power for the lights for our barracks, and also the steam heat from the boiler. And it was all rigged up just like it would have been aboard the ship.

I guess he had dropped the hint that it would be nice if the boys, while they were here, had a chance to drop in and see that. They'd never seen what it would be. Well, the Navy picked up on it right quick, and they saw to it that two of us spent a day in there. Out of all the time we were there, you could count on getting that with one other sailor. It really wasn't a big room--as wide as the one we're in, but then about three times as long as this would be in here.

Paul Stillwell: What, maybe about 50 or 60 feet long?

Mr. Logue: I'd guess so, because we were at the other end. When this happened, the door opened, and I thought all the gold in the Navy was coming in that door. There was admirals, captains, and pretty soon, here this tall, lanky guy come a-boiling out from amongst them. He looked down and saw us. He just took off and come down there, and those guys stayed back. They stayed at the door. We were at the other end. They just left him alone to come back there to us.

Came around and shook hands, and said, "My name's Henry Ford," just like you wouldn't know. We shook hands and told him who we were. Wanted to know where we were from and, "Yeah, I was in Wichita at such and such a time, and I was in St. Louis here just not very long ago," he told Jitler. He visited with us--oh, just as nice--just like you and I talking back and forth. Now, old Jitler was smarter than I was. At that time he had a farm in Georgia that he was raising soybeans on, and he was trying to develop plastics.

Now, back in those days plastics were the junkiest thing you could get your hands on. I mean, you buy a plastic toy--one day and it was gone. I mean, that's all the good they had out of plastics. I say that because Henry made the statement to us, "Boys, in five years you're going to see automobile bodies made out of plastic." Henry, you've been in it too long, you know. [Laughter] Of course, we didn't tell him that, but that was what was going on in our minds. We smiled and all that. "Well now," he said, "with this terrible war, who knows when we'll get in it or if we do or what?" He said it could make a difference because we were supplying a lot of stuff overseas.

Paul Stillwell: By now it was early 1941, I take it.

Mr. Logue: Yes. We're probably in March, April, and May of 1941.

Then he finally said, "Well now, because of that, it may take a little longer than five years, but you're going to see it in your lifetime." Nobody could be any more right than he was.

Paul Stillwell: Sure enough.

Mr. Logue: So, anyhow, it was a nice visit, and he turned to go. He shook hands, and so help me he told us as he shook hands, "Now, boys, if you ever see me anywhere, I don't care if I'm talking to the President of the United States, I want you to come up and interrupt me. Tell me who you are, where we met, and shake hands with me. I want you to promise you'll do that. Will you?" Of course, we promised. When he left, I told Jitler, "I don't think I'll interrupt the President. You can suit yourself." [Laughter]

Paul Stillwell: Who was the other man you were with?

Mr. Logue: Jitler was his last name.

Paul Stillwell: Do you remember his first name?

Mr. Logue: No, I sure don't. I wasn't with him a lot.

Paul Stillwell: I see.

Mr. Logue: But he was from St. Louis.

Paul Stillwell: Just happened to be with him that day.

Mr. Logue: Well, yes, we matched up because of alphabetical: J-K-L. That was as close as they could get alphabetically. They took us alphabetically, like, you know, the Navy did.

Paul Stillwell: What sort of class work or training did you have at Dearborn?

Mr. Logue: Well, at Dearborn we had an extension of what we had in class work, and we had a civilian instructor that was very good. In fact, that was the school that he built for us. We weren't in schools the Navy built. We were in Henry's classrooms.

Paul Stillwell: This was one of Henry Ford's machinists that was teaching you?

Mr. Logue: Yes. Well, see, Ford had that school for children of his own men, and that school had been going on for years. And, then, like a guy of Henry Ford's got killed or laid up and couldn't work or something like that, his kid could come in there and get free education and be insured of a job. So this was the class that we were in, with good instructors. Yes, we took each piece of equipment and understood how it went together and what it did and why it was needed and then some of the work that was done with it and things you could do with it. As I recall--now, again, I'm a lot of years, but these are things that kind of stick in with me.

Paul Stillwell: Did you wear your uniforms to class?

Mr. Logue: Yes. Well, dungarees. Course, that's all we would have anyhow.

Paul Stillwell: How much hands-on experience was in it?

Mr. Logue: Well, the morning was classroom, and the afternoon you were assigned a week at a time to a machine. And, of course, the main operator was there to teach you. He taught you, and he had you using that machine before the week was over.

Paul Stillwell: Like drill presses--

Mr. Logue: Lathes, and--

Paul Stillwell: Milling machines.

Mr. Logue: Grinders and things like that. Yes. Everything that was in that machine shop while we were there, we had a chance to spend time at each one of them coming around.

Paul Stillwell: I mentioned to you I interviewed a man named Joe Williams, who went through the school, and he said they put the Navy people first.* If you ruined a piece of metal stock, that wasn't important. The important thing was to learn.

Mr. Logue: That's right. That's exactly right. Yes, it was. And we were treated great. I have to say that. We were treated great.

Paul Stillwell: What examples do you have of that treatment?

Mr. Logue: Well, kind of like you said, and I know I'd goof up and hear, "Now, son, that's all right. Because everybody's got to learn, so come on." Just kind of that attitude: nobody jumping down your throat. Wasn't anything like that at all. It was strictly a

---

*See the Naval Institute oral history of Vice Admiral Joe Williams, Jr., USN (Ret.). Williams, who joined the Navy about the same time Mr. Logue did, was a machinist's mate prior to being commissioned as an officer.

patient--I know some of them probably would have liked to kick us right in the rear, but they didn't act like it. I mean, we were treated real good. Probably one of the nicest experiences that I had was Dearborn.

Paul Stillwell: You mentioned that you were at the top of your group at boot camp, and that's why you got to the school.

Mr. Logue: Well, I didn't know I was, but I guess--I didn't know.

Paul Stillwell: Did you get the feeling, though, that you were in there with people that had a lot of talent and aptitude for this machinist's mate training?

Mr. Logue: Yes, everybody that was in there was interested, and we would swap experiences in the barracks at night, you know: "Well, we did this and that and what about so-and-so and so on?" You would talk over what you did, and maybe they'd done it before you, and, "When we did it we did so and so and--" Yes, we shop talked quite a bit.

Paul Stillwell: Was there a high degree of motivation in there?

Mr. Logue: Yes, there was. I don't know of anybody that was in there for fun and games. Everybody I knew took it very seriously. Now, in our off time it was different. There were guys like myself. I had a little chord music, and they were working up a band. Where they got all their instruments I don't know, but they come up with trombones and clarinets and everything. They was getting kind of a little swing band going. They found out I could play a guitar, so they swung me in on that, and I got in with them for a while. I kind of got tired of it, so I quit.

They had fun doing that and lots of times we'd get around. They'd get the guitar and shove it in my face. They'd get around, and we'd sing together. Always a group, you know. Oh, let's sing this, or let's do that or something. Then we had liberty on weekends. I don't think we had it much during the week. Well, you could go to Dearborn, I guess.

But we'd generally catch a ride up to Dearborn and then catch the trolley over to Detroit and spend the weekend there, just to get away.

Paul Stillwell: What sorts of things would you do on liberty?

Mr. Logue: Well, about all we could do. They had cheap hotels, so we'd rent a room in a hotel and we'd eat a meal in a restaurant and that sort of thing. That's about all we could do.

Paul Stillwell: Well, you were drawing regular pay, so you could afford it.

Mr. Logue: Well, yes but not very big pay.

Paul Stillwell: Were you sending money home?

Mr. Logue: Yes, I was. I had an allotment made out right as soon as I could. Soon as I could get enough to go.

Paul Stillwell: Do you remember Ford's arranging dances for the sailors in this?

Mr. Logue: No. I don't remember anything like that now. But you want to remember, we were the third class to graduate out of that school. They were just starting, and so they probably improved a great deal after that. But it sounds like something he would have done. But at that time the only entertainment we had came from a strike while we there. [Laughter] Of course, that stopped our schooling too. We couldn't go across the fence over there, and we used to take sandwiches to the old boy over there that was patrolling the fence and all. We'd visit with him across the fence--one thing and another like that. But it only lasted a week, I think, and then we were all back again.

Paul Stillwell: I gather that the discipline in the barracks wasn't as strict as what you'd known at boot camp.

Mr. Logue: Not quite, but there was a discipline. I mean, we were expected to live out what we learned in there. We were expected to keep our clothes up. Now, we had bunks, of course, there. And we had a guard at night, and you took your turn whenever your guard duty came up.

And, oh yes, I guess I'd better tell you about Father Logue.

Paul Stillwell: Okay.

Mr. Logue: What in the world brought it on? Oh, I know. One evening, well, you know what it's like when the day's over, and you're getting ready to go ashore, getting ready to go on liberty and everybody's acting the fool, and we're in high spirits and all.

Paul Stillwell: That's right.

Mr. Logue: Okay. We were in the third barracks. They had just finished fourth one, and another group was going to come up. In fact, I think we were barracks C and then barracks D. We were just getting ready to leave to go on liberty, when they called on the speakers: "Father So-and-So," whatever his name was, we'll say Riley, "Father Riley will be hearing confessions in barracks D."

Now, we hadn't had any pastor of any kind there up until that time. But they say he's on the base now, and he will hear confessions in some room, whatever it was, in barracks D at such-and-such, 9:00 o'clock that night, I think, or something like that. And old mouthy me, of course, I was feeling great like everybody else, and I said, "Well, Father Logue will hold confessions in the shower room tomorrow morning at 8:00 o'clock." Brother, that stuck. I was Father Logue for the rest of the time I was in the Navy. [Laughter] They cut it down to Pappy sometimes, but--

Paul Stillwell: You were just trying to make fun of it.

Mr. Logue: Oh, yes. I should have brought the pictures, but I didn't think there'd be any use for them. These guys took pictures. I had a raincoat put on backwards. I had my white hat folded in a certain way that it kind of looked like a priest's hat, and this old boy's on his knees in front of me with his hands like this.

Paul Stillwell: Folded his hands.

Mr. Logue: I've got my hand on him, and I'm holding The Bluejackets' Manual.

Paul Stillwell: Like it's a Bible. [Laughter]

Mr. Logue: Yes. So we had fun with it. We had our 50th wedding anniversary three years ago. A little buddy from down in Tennessee, little Tommy Gregg that I went through with him--and he was at the school, incidentally, and we went to the same ship. He and I stayed on the New York together until Okinawa, and they had to take him off. But, anyhow, they came to our 50th wedding anniversary, and I was still Pappy Logue.

Paul Stillwell: [Laughter] Was any of this training geared toward shipboard propulsion plants?

Mr. Logue: No, it wasn't, and it would have helped. I think that was the first great letdown, because we left there when we graduated and went back to Great Lakes, and they sent us to Philadelphia. Great Scott, they put us in a barracks there for a month. All we did was get out and go on liberty every night. There wasn't a thing to do. It was an old barracks at that. We kept it cleaned up and one thing and another.

Paul Stillwell: So this is about May or June?

Mr. Logue: This was June, and then toward the end of June they shipped us up to Newport, Rhode Island, and we went aboard a repair ship there just briefly, about a week, until the Texas came in. Then they put us on the Texas, and then after a week on the

Texas, they put us over on the New Mexico, and then a week after that they put us on the Mississippi.

Paul Stillwell: What do you remember about these individual battleships as you went through them?

Mr. Logue: The best treatment we got was on the Texas.

Paul Stillwell: Why do you say that?

Mr. Logue: Well, they accepted us more. We were the lowest of the low. We were just coming aboard out of a school--out of a training and so forth--but they at least showed us more courtesy, and they were more helpful to us. Some of them could get pretty nasty on some of those other ships, especially the Mississippi. Just the difference in the ships, I suppose.

Paul Stillwell: What sort of work did they have you doing in these various ships?

Mr. Logue: Oh, help this guy, help that guy, or something like that. I don't know. And again we had to take our hammocks, and all we could do was spread our hammock out on the deck underneath somebody's bunk and sleep that way, and we didn't have any money. We hadn't been paid. Now, the New York came in then, and after the Mississippi we went to the New York, but there's something interesting, at least to me.* You remember the story, The Winds of War?†

Paul Stillwell: Sure.

---

*USS New York (BB-34) was commissioned 15 April 1914. She had a standard displacement of 27,000 tons, was 573 feet long, and 95 feet in the beam. Her top speed was 21 knots. She was armed with ten 14-inch guns, 16 5-inch guns, and eight 3-inch guns. She was eventually decommissioned in 1946 after service in World War II.
†Herman Wouk's novel The Winds of War followed a fictitious Navy captain named Victor "Pug" Henry, who in the story was President Franklin D. Roosevelt's naval aide in the period leading up to U.S. involvement in World War II. The book was made into a television mini-series in the early 1980s.

Mr. Logue: Did you see the movie?

Paul Stillwell: Yes.

Mr. Logue: Now, this probably would have went clear past you, but when this what's-his-name, the actor, played the part of the captain--

Paul Stillwell: Pug Henry.

Mr. Logue: Yes, Pug Henry. When Pug was over in England and they were talking about radar and he mentioned the word--well, they were testing radar on the New York. That's where she was when I was back there in Newport, waiting on her to come in. And that was rather interesting to me, because that was the first I'd heard. I knew she was out there testing radar, but I never thought about it being in conjunction.

Paul Stillwell: She was not that far away from the Bismarck.* The Bismarck made her sortie in May of '41, and she wasn't really close, but she was at sea at the same time in the North Atlantic.

Mr. Logue: I see. Well, we made four trips across the North Atlantic as leader of convoys. But, anyhow, that was later.

Paul Stillwell: On the Mississippi did they just treat you completely like outsiders?

Mr. Logue: Yes, they did. They really did. They were haughty, and you couldn't find a friendly face or a thing--

---

*In May 1941, the German battleship Bismarck, accompanied by the cruiser Prinz Eugen, entered the open Atlantic as a prelude to operating as a surface raider. In a gun duel on 24 May against the British, she sank the Hood and damaged the Prince of Wales. The Bismarck herself was damaged on the 26th by British torpedo planes and sunk on the 27th by gunfire from the British battleships Rodney and King George V.

Paul Stillwell: They put you on working parties and so forth?

Mr. Logue: Yes, and then, of course, you didn't mind that part of it. You just kind of like to expected a little camaraderie or something like that, but you couldn't find it there.

Paul Stillwell: So it was just the atmosphere more than anything.

Mr. Logue: Yes, that's right. New Mexico wasn't as really as nice as the Texas boys were, but they were sure better than Mississippi. Funny how that will hang in your mind and all. That was just their way, I mean. So then New York came into Newport, and they took us aboard.

Paul Stillwell: Do you remember what month that was?

Mr. Logue: Yes, August of 1941. And here's where I got my first jolt. I'd trained to be a machinist, I thought, and I went into the forward engine room. Now, I've got to get you straight if you don't see it. There was only two battleships that had triple-expansion reciprocating steam engines, and that was the New York and the Texas.

Paul Stillwell: The Oklahoma had one too.

Mr. Logue: Well, we didn't know that. We were told that they was the only two. Fair enough.

Paul Stillwell: She was on the other coast. She was over in the Pacific.

Mr. Logue: Yes, I knew she was when we went around there. Well, this happened back in--let's see, one of them was built in 1912 and one in 1914.[*] I think the New York in '14 if I'm not mistaken.

---

[*] USS Texas (BB-35) was commissioned 12 March 1914.

Paul Stillwell: Right around there.

Mr. Logue: Were you ever aboard either one of them?

Paul Stillwell: I've been aboard the Texas. She's down near Galveston.

Mr. Logue: Were you down in the engine rooms?

Paul Stillwell: I don't think so.

Mr. Logue: Well. I was going to say, to feature you've got to see two big shafts coming out one on a side and each one of them attached to an engine, which was different from a lot of them. Some of them had three shafts coming out, but turbines. But, then, these you just have two, and it's connected--they're four-cylinder--they got first your HP and your IP and then your two LPs.* Okay. This was all very fine, but I'd been trained to be a machinist. I thought I was going in the machine shop, and the first thing I got was duty down there in the forward engine room, and that's as close to the machine shop as I ever got. So I stayed in there for about three months. And they were good guys. They were good, and they were trying to be good to us and all, but I wasn't enjoying that. Wasn't what I wanted to learn and--now, my brother, he stuck through it and got those jobs I told you about.

Paul Stillwell: Tell me about working with those triple-expansion engines. That's fascinating.

Mr. Logue: Well, you had about 450 pounds of steam coming in--now, the destroyers they said had 600, but we had about 450 pounds of steam coming in. Well, you had a cylinder--I'm going to say about that big around, which we called the HP--that's your high pressure--

---

*HP--high pressure; IP--intermediate pressure; LP--low pressure.

Paul Stillwell: About a foot and a half.

Mr. Logue: Something like that--18 inches across. This is from memory now and a long time ago. You got one that's about 18 inches, let's say, in diameter, and that's where your first steam goes, and it expands. But it's got a lot more expansion left. So it goes from there over to the intermediate pressure, IP. And it's, oh, quite a bit bigger, like this.

Paul Stillwell: Two or three feet.

Mr. Logue: Yes. And it expands again, and then it goes to your two LPs, and those jewels I think you could put about four or five men standing on top of the piston of them. They were that big. The steam expanded again, and that's when they went out then over to your hot well. And they run it through the grease extractors and so forth and cleaned all the grease and everything out of it, back to the boiler room to make steam out of it.

Paul Stillwell: And these pistons are hooked on to a crankshaft.

Mr. Logue: Just like a car. That's right. And you could see them old pistons and shafts going up and down. See your crankshaft was down there, going round and round, when you were under way, you bet.

Paul Stillwell: I've been in triple-expansion plant in an old Liberty ship, and they had little oil cups on the sides that you had to squirt oil into.

Mr. Logue: No, not so much. We had a little oil can--I'm trying to think what that was for--and you dumped it every once in a while. I don't remember--maybe they did. I'll tell you. I was only in there three months, and most of my work under way was the grease extractors. Are you familiar with those?

Paul Stillwell: No. Please tell me.

Mr. Logue: All right. Grease extractors are cylinders with a head on top with bolts that you had to tighten, and you tightened them with a sledge hammer. I mean, it had them big deals you put on that come out to a point, and you hit that to tighten it that hard. Okay. Had a gasket, but down inside of there, there was a copper cylinder full of holes. And you pulled that out; course, you pulled it out with a rope, because it would be boiling hot. And it had the toweling on it, and you cut the cords of that toweling, which it had extracted grease on that toweling. Threw that down and got some new toweling, wrapped it around this porous cylinder, and with a needle and heavy string--thread--you did a fast job of sewing to keep it on there, and you put that down in and you headed it up again. Then you changed your valves back over to it so the steam would run through there. And when you're under way only 15 minutes, and then you change them every 15 minutes. And there's two of us on there all the time, and that's one watch that you only had to stand for two hours.

Paul Stillwell: That would get old in a hurry.

Mr. Logue: Oh, you know it did.

Paul Stillwell: How hot was it in there?

Mr. Logue: Oh, hot. Real hot. Real hot. It really was. I don't know what the temperature was.

Paul Stillwell: Over 100 probably.

Mr. Logue: Oh, yes. Much. It really was. Because you were up on top, and that was worse yet than down on the floor. There was only a catwalk up there where these things were that we were working on, so after about three months of it and some of my buddies--well, this little Tommy Gregg I was telling you about that came back to the party, he was in the E division, and he had tipped me off that they were wanting some men over there.

So I went immediately to the E division officer and talked to him, and it happened to be Admiral Thomas C. Hart's little boy, Junior.[*] Tassie Hart--bless his heart, he died before I got out of the Navy.[†] I hated to hear that. He was a splendid man. He was really a fine man. He was an ensign at that time and E division officer.[‡] He was very kind to me but firm like an officer would be, and he said, "Well." First, he wanted to know why I wanted to come over.

So I told him, "I trained to be a machinist, and I'm down there in the engine room, and there's nothing about it that I'm interested in carrying over. I want to get into a trade that I can learn."

He said, "That sounds logical." So he said, "Let's see what we can do." I was new in the Navy and I went about it wrong, but I had an excellent division officer in the M division too. Lieutenant Baumberger came down, and he said, "Logue, they tell me that you want to get out of this division."[§]

I said, "Not so much the division, Mr. Baumberger, but I want to get into the electrical part of the ship." I said, "I trained to be a machinist, and I should have known better, but I know your little machine shop up there. You can't put all of us in there." And I said, "The engine room work carries me nothing and doesn't offer me much on the outside." And I said, "I really --"

"Well," he said, "you don't have any trouble with any of the guys in there?"

"As far as I'm concerned, no. I've got good friends in--" In fact I got into a quartet down there in M division, and we used to go around and sing. Even on the beach.

So he said, "Well, if that's the way you feel--you really want to go over, I'll do what I can for you."

I said, "Well I really appreciate it."

He said, "We want people happy around here if we can." Now, those were good officers, and I think most of them were. But, of course, once in a while the ones you'd remember were the ones who weren't so great.

---

[*] Ensign Thomas Comins Hart, USN. His father, Thomas Charles Hart, was a four-star admiral then serving as Commander in Chief U.S. Asiatic Fleet.
[†] Hart, as a lieutenant commander, died of leukemia 17 June 1945 at San Francisco. He was 28 years old.
[‡] E division handled the electrical equipment on board the ship.
[§] Lieutenant (junior grade) Walter H. Baumberger, USN.

Paul Stillwell: Baumberger wound up a three-star admiral.

Mr. Logue: Did he really?

Paul Stillwell: Yes, he did.

Mr. Logue: Oh, you knew him then.

Paul Stillwell: Red Baumberger, I think he was called.

Mr. Logue: Yes, sir. That's right. Well, he was an excellent man and he was a good military man. There wasn't any question about it. I mean, he carried himself well and all.

Paul Stillwell: He was an academy graduate.

Mr. Logue: I imagine he was. Well, anyhow, they went up to the log room, and a few days later they called me up to the log room.[*] There was Mr. Baumberger, and there was Mr. Hart, and there was Commander--I can't think of his name. Lieutenant Commander Haycock was the assistant chief engineer, and this guy was the chief engineer.[†] And he sat in the chair about like this.

Paul Stillwell: That was a lot of rank for you to be confronting.

Mr. Logue: Tell me about it. [Laughter] I went up, and I wondered why'd I ever started this, see. He said, "What makes you think you can be an electrician?"

And I said, "Well, sir, I see a lot of guys that have become an electrician, and I'm a guy, too, and I just feel like I can. I'm interested in it."

"Well," he said, "you know anything about it? Did you ever have any experience in it?"

---

[*] The engineering log room was essentially the headquarters office for the engineering department and the storage site for engineering logs.
[†] Lieutenant Commander Warren E. Haycock, USNR.

I'd always been taught that if you're going to go for a job, if you can reach back and grab anything you know to put into it, why, you'd better do it. I said, "Well, my brother had an electrical shop and a battery shop."

"Oh, you're one of these guys that come out and kicked the battery and said you need a new one." I thought the best thing in the world for me to say was nothing, so I just smiled. Finally he turned around to Mr. Hart, and he says, "Take him. He's yours." Just like that, so I was in E division.

I thanked Mr. Baumberger for his help; he was very nice about it. And I thanked Mr. Hart for taking me. So my first task then--you were supposed to do mess cook or compartment cleaning or something like that. Well, they already had theirs set up. So E division was supposed to send one down to the chiefs' quarters, and I went down and worked under a coxswain down there and got along real well with him.* He was real nice. Remember what I said about deck force and engineering--but when you're working together, that's a different story.

Paul Stillwell: Please tell me about mess cooking.

Mr. Logue: I never got into that. I thank goodness I never had to, but then we had--we had the old family type on that ship. We had the tables set up, and they brought the food down to us and we set around in our own compartment and ate--at first. Now, they changed it toward the end of my time there.

Paul Stillwell: These were the ten-man tables.

Mr. Logue: Yes, right. And so we had mess cooks that would do that for a while. How long did they have to do that? A month, I think, or something like that.

Paul Stillwell: But they got tips, too, didn't they? Did you pitch in for their payday.

---

*Coxswain at that time was the E-4 level of the boatswain's mate rating. There was then no boatswain's mate third class as there is now.

Mr. Logue: Sometimes, yes, sometimes. If they come across, I mean, and did like they should. So they'd fight for the tips, but the compartment cleaners would get no tips. They just cleaned the compartment every day.

Paul Stillwell: Oh, so you were compartment cleaner at first?

Mr. Logue: In the chiefs' quarters, yes. But after I finished that up, then they put me as a striker in the light shop. Are you familiar with the light shop and about what that would be?

Paul Stillwell: Well, please tell me. I know you're going to keep the lights going.

Mr. Logue: Well, this was mainly it. You had responsibility for every light on that ship. And that meant running lights, that meant all the navigation lights, everything on the bridge, anything--in fact, we had fighting lights, and there's a story on that before it's over with.

Paul Stillwell: Okay.

Mr. Logue: We had not only that but any of the light electric motors and things like that. The power shop had the big heavy motors and that sort of stuff.

Paul Stillwell: Like on turrets.

Mr. Logue: Yes, turrets, the cranes, and things like that. The IC room was your internal communications. We had what we called ship's service telephones, which were just like the ones you have at home or one we had there on the farm. Then we had sound power.[*] That was a tremendous thing, as far as I was concerned. I don't know why it didn't go farther than it did.

---

[*]Sound-powered telephones require no battery or external source of electrical current to carry voice transmissions from station to another. The speaker's voice activates a diaphragm inside the phone speaker that generates the current to operate the system.

Paul Stillwell: The IC men took care of those phones, didn't they?

Mr. Logue: Yes, they took care of that. And then your distribution was your distribution boards. You didn't have a big crew there, but you had to have people who did maintenance on it and all. But we kept a man on watch on the boards at all times--24 hours a day. Now, your crew took care of it from the time we come down from quarters after 8:00 o'clock muster, then the crew took over. And whoever was on watch would go to his daily duties. But then, starting at 4:00 o'clock in the evening, why, then the crew went off, and whoever had the watch from 4:00 to 8:00 and so on around, and you were posted on watch, so I stood many a watch on those boards.

So then your forward board was your master board. That was where the command post would be. Like I explained, the division officer would be up there during general quarters, battle, maneuvers, or anything like that. And then the men on the after board simply got their orders from the forward board. And if they wanted any switches pulled back there or thrown in or something, why, they weren't allowed to do anything of that sort without authorization from the forward board. The forward board man had it on his shoulders. He was trained to do that, but, of course, you didn't get to be in charge of the forward board until you got to be at least second class electrician's mate. You knew what you were doing, or you didn't get on there. So this was what that was about.

Paul Stillwell: There was a lot of professionalism in those prewar sailors.

Mr. Logue: Well, there had to be. I mean, it was an old battleship, and it was a direct current battleship. The only alternating current we had we made with the motor generator sets. And that was for the equipment that we had on there. This was a World War I battleship. They'd never changed. I'm getting a little ahead of myself, but to give you an illustration, the first trip we went over as leader of convoys, we had four .50-caliber machine guns, and that was all the antiaircraft we had.* They were all over the place, so we had a lot of upbringing to get those things to where they were really usable.

Paul Stillwell: What are the disadvantages of direct current?

Mr. Logue: Well, you can produce alternating current cheaper, and actually, when you're producing through generators or that [unclear] you're making both alternating and--in other words, you're getting direct current, but you're getting two different direct currents with each other, is the best way I can put it to you. You're losing one when you cut it down to direct. In those days they didn't have the way of bringing that thing around and joining like they can do nowadays. Back then you lost part of it and saved the DC direct part, because this came from batteries and stuff like that and they're evolving electricity and therefore--

In the days it was built the main thing was direct current. That's all they needed. That's the best answer I can give you. And it would cost a tremendous amount to have taken all those DC generators out of there and put in alternators. They didn't think on a ship that old that it was worth it, so they put on MG sets.† The only place that you had to have it was on some of your newer equipment that required it, like your gyrocompass and some other equipment on the ship that I might not have been totally familiar with but required the AC current. It was especially that way on the bridge, so they would get MG sets in logical places and be able to feed the alternating current where it was absolutely necessary. Some of your gun firing was involved in that and so forth.

Paul Stillwell: They had already made one big change. They had changed from coal to oil for the propulsion.

Mr. Logue: That's true. We didn't have any coal; we were burning oil. That's correct. They got there before I did, thank goodness, or I'd have been doing this as a machinist.

---
*The 1941 edition of Jane's Fighting Ships credits the New York with eight 3-inch/50-caliber antiaircraft guns and eight .50-caliber machine guns that could be used against planes.
† MG-motor generator.

Paul Stillwell: Shoveling coal is the motion you're making.

Mr. Logue: [Laughter] Yes. Yes, indeed. I enjoyed it. I went on as a striker, and usually you had to be a third class. The ship was divided into areas, and each third class was assigned the responsibility to keep up all the electrical equipment in there that had to do with the light shop. If they had lights out, or if they had a piece of machinery in there that wasn't operating or needed it, and you didn't--you make your rounds, and if it goes down, why, they call the shop. They get a hold of you, and you go up there and do it. Okay. Then they give you a striker. Well, that's how you learn. You follow that third class around, and he shows you what you're doing and how to do it and what the responsibilities are, and that's how you first begin.

Of course, you had to study from not only your A to N but also your electrical book until you can pass an examination with a pretty high grade before they would give you that.* They handed them out pretty lively later on, but back then you earned every grade you got.† Then I made my third class and I got my area.

Paul Stillwell: Well, now that rating was different from machinist's mate. That started at second class, I think.

Mr. Logue: Yes. The third class electrician, and the fireman first class really were on the same level as far as pay was concerned. The only difference is the third class is a petty officer and the fireman first isn't.

Paul Stillwell: So you got an advantage that way going to electrician's mate on that.

Mr. Logue: Never even thought about it at the time, but that's right. That's true. There wasn't much of an advantage when you had to go take on shore patrol duty in town.

---

*The A to N subjects dealt with general military and naval topics, as opposed to the specific requirements of the electrician's mate rating.
†Advancement in the prewar Navy was painfully slow. It became much more rapid with the onset of war and the need for huge growth in the size of the fleet and the concomitant enlisted population.

Paul Stillwell: [Laughter] You probably were treated with more respect.

Mr. Logue: No.

Paul Stillwell: No?

Mr. Logue: No. No, no. You were a big horse's rear end for doing what you did. Run some guy in or something. What are you going to do? You had to.

Paul Stillwell: What sort of operations was the New York involved in during the latter half of 1941?

Mr. Logue: We operated out of Newport, Rhode Island, mostly up around New England. About all we'd do was go out and maneuver, and that was to be able to exercise every department of the ship. They exercised the gunnery out in the waters away, and each one of us had our own job down below, irregardless of where we were at. We operated in and out.

I wonder if you'd be interested in a particular liberty that I took with a couple of guys, friends.

Paul Stillwell: Sure.

Mr. Logue: Now look, hey, we didn't have much money. And you're not used to being on a ship all that long, and you're tickled to death to get over on the beach. I have seen the time when I was on the beach years later I'd want to get back on the ship, but then that's another thing. Anyhow, we went over in Newport, and we walked around. That was about all we could afford to do. We were down to just cents almost, but we didn't want to go back to the ship. Didn't want to sleep in the darn bunk; we wanted to stay over there on the beach. So where are you going to sleep? We don't have money enough to get a bunk anywhere, and if they had a YMCA there then, we didn't know it.[*] So, anyhow, I said,

---

[*]YMCA--Young Men's Christian Association.

"Let's go to the jail and see if they'll let us have a bunk." [Laughter] So we went in there and asked them. "Why, we aren't running no hotel in here," was their answer.

One of our guys said, "Well, if we went out and threw a rock through the window, would you put us in then?"

"Yeah, I think we would, but we might not let you out either." So we hemmed and hawed. Finally, he said, "Well, I'll tell you, boys. If you don't have a place and you want to, why, you can sleep on one of those benches in that room in there." So all three of us spent the night in the jail on those benches. The darn shifts would come in and wake us up, "Hey, these guys are trying to sleep."

"Oh, oh, oh." But we put up with it for the night. I tell you, you're crazy. You aren't going to believe this, but the next morning it seemed to me like we had just enough money left to buy a can of pork and beans and a loaf of bread. We went out in the park, and that was our breakfast. [Laughter] Well, we finally went back aboard ship, and when we did, why, they had a lot better food than we'd been eating. So that was just one of the things--going up and trying to get a jail cell so we could sleep.

Paul Stillwell: Did the ship moor to a pier there or anchor?

Mr. Logue: No, we anchored out mostly at Newport.

Paul Stillwell: So you had to run boats.

Mr. Logue: Yes. And then another time we were in Taunton, Massachusetts; we were operating out of Fall River then. This was almost kind of New England area that we just stayed in for a while. I don't know what the heck we were doing. I didn't go topside. I was just doing my job down below. I think we were just maneuvering around, training, and trying to keep on top of things. We were getting good training then. Guys like me, anyhow, were. And so when we were there at Fall River--it was a good little old town--but we decided we'd hitchhike over to Taunton. A couple of ladies picked us up in their car and took us over to Taunton. One of them got a little fresh, but then they decided they weren't as fresh as they thought they were, so they let us out in Taunton. [Laughter]

Paul Stillwell: How did you discourage their freshness?

Mr. Logue: I didn't discourage their freshness.

Paul Stillwell: Oh.

Mr. Logue: The other lady did. [Laughter] There was three of us. The same old three. We went over there, and so they let us out. I used to drink a little. Not a lot. I think in my life I was probably drunk about twice, but I used to with an old buddy of mine named John Diamond. We'd go over and get what he called a golden glow, and then when the glow ceased, we'd get a little more. "Keep a golden glow," he'd always call it. But we went over, but these two guys, they soused. They went out. They got drunk.

Paul Stillwell: What were you drinking?

Mr. Logue: I never liked beer, and I very seldom ever drank it. I probably drank mixed drinks or wine or something like that. Didn't care too much for wine. I didn't mind whiskey if it was cut down a little bit. I didn't want straight whiskey very bad. Like I said, didn't drink a lot but enough to get happy, so to speak, and kind of be with the guys. But, these guys, buddies of mine, got loaded and drunk.

Well, this is a little New England town, and that didn't go over one bit. It wasn't a big town at all; it was a little town. We didn't know what we was getting into, so here come a policeman. He was going to run them in. I was all right, but he was going to run them in. I said, "Ah, come on. Come on. Let me get them out of here. I'll get them out of here."

"Well, get them out of here," he said. "We can't have them on the streets like this. This isn't going to do at all." Both were singing, both of them different songs, and I got this guy's arm around me and this guy that way like that, had them on. I took off with them like a football player, and they're a-singing and a-carrying on, you know. I told them, "Shut up, shut up, you crazy nuts." They didn't pay any attention to me.

Well, I started across the park, and he had told me that they was a bus stop over there. I thought, "Well, that's good enough." But he didn't trust me. He followed me over there to see that I went there. So when the bus come along, why, we got on and took it to Fall River, Massachusetts. I took them back to the back of the bus and set them down. They sang, both of them, at the top of their voices. I thought the driver was going to put us off. And people were a-having a fit, you know. The driver didn't have a thing to say.

So, finally, we were the last two left on the bus heading in for Fall River, so he stopped the bus and come back, and I thought, "Oh, oh, here's where we're going to get off." He come back, and being as I was the only sober one, he talked to me and he said, "Now, we're going to hit some curves and some rough roads. If the boys get sick and if they heave on the floor, don't think a thing about it. "This is the last trip. We'll just take it in and clean it."

I said, "Hey, Mister, you're the nicest man I've talked to today."

"No," he said, "that's all right. Just wanted to so you wouldn't worry about it if it happened." So I hung on to them, and we got out into Fall River and we went into the YMCA this time. I took their billfolds and anything that looked like it was valuable of any kind and stuck it under my pillow, along with mine. They finally woke up with heads about like this and both started looking for their billfolds, saying, "I've been robbed!"

I said, "You ain't kidding. It was me too." [Laughter]

Paul Stillwell: Father Logue.

Mr. Logue: Yes. I had those two experiences, but we lived through them all, as far as that's concerned. But then we did function around there in New England.

Paul Stillwell: Did you travel along with other ships? Were they in formation?

Mr. Logue: I couldn't tell you that. We were down below, and if I knew about it I've forgotten that.

Paul Stillwell: What was the sensation when the guns fired?

Mr. Logue: Well, you could feel it, depending on which guns. You could hear the small ones. I'd better explain. We had 5-inch, we had 3-inch, and we had those four .50-caliber machine guns.

Paul Stillwell: And you had 14-inch in the turrets.

Mr. Logue: Had 14-inch in five turrets--ten guns. They were two guns to the turret, where the new ships had three.

Paul Stillwell: Right.

Mr. Logue: And they only had nine, but we were 14-inch, and Texas was 14-inch. The Arkansas was 12-inch. They were afloat, boy, and they were in on those invasions too. But, anyhow, I know very little about what went on topside, really, at that point and probably from then on, except what you'd hear from up there. But all I know was that we maneuvered down in that area for quite some time, and finally then we went up to Argentia Bay, Newfoundland, and we operated out of there. We all grew beards, even me. I cut mine off, and shaving it off like to killed me. I did not shave it off. I just stopped shaving and pulled it out by the roots, I think. That was the end of my beards, I tell you.

Paul Stillwell: What inspired you grow a beard?

Mr. Logue: Everybody did. I don't know. It was out of the States, see, and the old man tolerated it. So everybody on the ship, I think, had a beard.

Paul Stillwell: Who was the old man? Do you remember?

Mr. Logue: Captain J. G. Ware.* I had four captains. I don't know how many of them

---

*Captain James G. Ware, USN, commanded the New York, 1941-42.

you might have known. The next one was Scotty Umsted.* He was the best fighting skipper we ever had. We had very little to do with him. He had very little to do with the crew. He turned that over to Commander Hansen, but he ran that ship and, I mean, he knew how to do it.† Then we had Kemp C. Christian, and I didn't enjoy him quite as much for various reasons.‡ Then the last one was Grayson B. Carter, and he was a dandy too.§ I don't know what kind of a fighting skipper he was, because he didn't come aboard till after Okinawa, but he was an awful nice captain. He was good to the crew and all.

But, anyhow, we went up there. The crew called the captain Mother Ware, bless his heart. He was kind of like that, I guess.

Paul Stillwell: In what way?

Mr. Logue: Well, he would kind of mother the boys and, be real kind to them, you know. I don't know. I never had that much experience, but I'd just hear him referred to as that, you know. He maybe didn't deserve it, but they thought he did; it was a title. But nobody disliked him. Don't misunderstand me there.

We maneuvered in and out of port, and then we had boxing matches and wrestling matches up there for sports--stuff to do on the deck. Finally, on our last time out of there, the poor old man ran that thing aground, and he tore one gash on the starboard side of that ship. I thought we'd lose her. We had to counterflood the port side, and we closed, of course, every watertight thing we could find around there.

Paul Stillwell: What did he run aground on?

Mr. Logue: I have no idea. Like I say, you don't get much of that, but we know that it happened. So they pulled the Texas in right along the side of us, because there were subs out there. We weren't in the war yet, but you never knew when one of those silly guys would do something, especially if it had a crippled ship like that going in. So they pulled

---

*Captain Scott Umsted, USN, commanded the New York, 1942-43.
†Commander George L. Hansen, USN, commanded the New York, 1946.
‡Captain Kemp C. Christian, USN, commanded the New York, 1943-45.
§Captain Grayson B. Carter, USN, commanded the New York, 1945-46.

the Texas right in beside us, between us and anything out there. They drug us down to Norfolk, put us in dry dock immediately, and went to work on us. And then it was Pearl Harbor.*

Paul Stillwell: Did you go ashore in Newfoundland at all?

Mr. Logue: No. And it was pretty hard to take. I don't think anybody was afraid.

Paul Stillwell: How did you get the news of the Japanese attack?

Mr. Logue: I was coming out of the theater in Norfolk on Sunday afternoon, and they was screaming it on the newspaper, "Pearl Harbor Bombed"--"Bombed Pearl Harbor"--"Bombed Pearl Harbor"--and, you know, it was just the natural thing to do. Everybody went back to their ship. It was way early, but you all went back to your ship. Just drawn there.

Paul Stillwell: Sense of duty.

Mr. Logue: Well, I suppose. And you wanted to be with your gang. You wanted to be with your people. I mean, if there was anything we could do, we wanted to be there, I guess. I don't know. Anyhow, we went back, and all of us collected in our own compartments,. They had these radio speakers in each compartment there, and, of course, we heard Roosevelt's speech then.†

Paul Stillwell: He talked to Congress and asked for the declaration of war.

---

*On 7 December 1941, the Imperial Japanese Navy launched a strike from six aircraft carriers against Pacific Fleet warships moored in Pearl Harbor Hawaii. All told, the force of some 350 planes--fighters, dive-bombers, torpedo planes, and high-level bombers--wreaked heavy destruction and killed more than 2,000 military personnel. The attack inflamed American public opinion and led to a U.S. declaration of war against Japan the following day.
†On Monday, 8 December, President Franklin D. Roosevelt addressed a joint session of Congress about the events of the preceding day. He began with the compelling words, "Yesterday, December 7, 1941, a date which will live in infamy . . ."

Mr. Logue: Yes, that's right. So we didn't know what would happen. Of course, we weren't going anywhere. We were in dry dock. But I tell you--now, I know how ridiculous this sounds, but we were young guys, and we were upset. I mean, we were upset. We would have taken that ship out to whip the whole Jap Navy if they'd have let us, if we could have got the ship out. I mean, we knew better than that. But then, that's just the way you felt.

Paul Stillwell: That feeling was all over the country.

Mr. Logue: I'm sure it was.

Paul Stillwell: People were showing up at recruiting offices and what have you.

Mr. Logue: Wasn't that something? Well, anyhow, another thing that was pretty touchy for me was this Captain Ware before they took him off of it. He decided, "Well, don't tell when these boys will ever get leave again, and this ship isn't going anywhere for a while." So he instructed his division officer--no, maybe it was Umsted, I believe it was. Because they got Captain Ware off of there.

Paul Stillwell: Because of the grounding?

Mr. Logue: Now, I would suppose. I mean, how would I know for sure? But I just know they took him off right away after that, and then Scotty gave instructions to all the division officers that a certain percent of their crew could have a five-day leave. All they could do was just put all the names in a hat and pull out the number, whatever it came to.

Well, I never was lucky in my life and would you believe, they drew my name out? And there I am in Norfolk, Virginia, and five days, and I live in Wichita, Kansas. I couldn't begin to make that in a train, and I had no money for a plane. So I kept trying to give it to somebody else, but you know what those guys did? Went around and took up a collection. They got me money enough to get a plane ticket home. But that's the kind of guys they were. That's the kind of guys you were shipping with.

Paul Stillwell: These were guys in your division?

Mr. Logue: Yes, sir. And they were guys that you could trust.

Paul Stillwell: What percentage of the crew got leave, would you say?

Mr. Logue: I don't think more than about--I'm going to say 25-30%.

Paul Stillwell: So it was a real privilege.

Mr. Logue: You bet, you bet. So I got to go home, and I felt bad about it in a way, but they wouldn't have it any other way. All I could do was cry a little and thank them. On the way out it was snowing. I took a bus out to the airport, and they grounded the planes. There was a guy dressed in a business suit and he said, "Sailor, what are you going to do tonight?"

I said, "I'm going to sleep right here on this bench."

"Well," he said, "there ought to be something better than that." He said, "I just had a room in the"--oh, what was that fancy hotel in Norfolk?

Paul Stillwell: The Chamberlin?

Mr. Logue: No. It was a big one, though. He said, "I just had a room there." He said, "I'll call, and if they haven't let it, why, we'll go back and sleep there." And, sure enough, they hadn't, and, by George, he got a taxi and took me back, and I was real impressed with the guy. When we got ready to go to bed, he said, "If you'll excuse me please," and he knelt down beside of his bed and had prayer before he got into bed, which impressed me greatly.

I grew up in a Christian home, and it took me several years later to get back on the stick, but, thank God, I finally did, but that's another story. But he took me out to the airport then the next day. We took the same plane up as far as Washington, D.C., and he went on Philadelphia and I went on to--one more stop, I forget where it was. Oh, it must have been Kansas City. And then down to Wichita. Took me 14 hours to get from Norfolk to Wichita and this last spring it took me six hours to get from Kansas City to--oh, north of San Francisco--big city there in California. I can't remember. Anyhow, we went back there to see my sister, and it took six hours--what a difference.

Paul Stillwell: Yes.

Mr. Logue: But then I had, of course, the round-trip ticket, and then we had a few days there with Mickey and my Dad and came back again.

Paul Stillwell: Did you get to see your future wife when you were there?

Mr. Logue: Oh, you know it. You know it. There's going to be an interesting part come up on that pretty soon.

Paul Stillwell: All right.

Mr. Logue: But, anyhow, I got back, and they finally got that ship out of there, and they sent us up to New York and we went into--I guess it's the East River, that's the big one isn't it?

Paul Stillwell: That leads up to the Brooklyn Navy Yard.

Mr. Logue: Oh, it does? Well, what's the one goes to the piers. Is that the North River?

Paul Stillwell: Well, it's the Hudson, but they call that part the North River off the piers. It's on the west side of the city.

Mr. Logue: Okay. That's right. Okay, well that's the one, because we always had Pier 51. I don't know why, but we did. We went up there and had some liberties up there--one thing and another--I think while they were trying to get organized in what they were going to do. It turned out to be convoy leaders. We'd run around 120 to 130 ships in our convoys. We were the leaders. They had three destroyers that constantly circled us. We couldn't go very fast, because this was before Henry Kaiser out in San Francisco had all his fleet built, you know.* He was working. And so we had old banana boats and anything else they could put together. And your top speed was generally around 10 to 12 knots because of what you're pulling. And it was kind of hairy.

It so happened that very trip we went to Reykjavik, Iceland. Then the British came out and met the convoys and took them on in. But the rest of them--the other three--all went straight into England, only we discharged them and we went around to Greenock, Scotland, and that's where we anchored. Had wonderful liberty there in Scotland. Those people were wonderful. I can't say enough for them.

Paul Stillwell: Please tell me about the liberties.

Mr. Logue: We took our boat over, and we had to be back to the ship by midnight, but they let us go at 1:00 o'clock in the afternoon. We went over and, oh, those people, couldn't have been more wonderful. You couldn't believe them. They were cheerful, they were polite, they were everything that people ought to be for all the suffering that they had gone through.

We went to Glasgow for liberty, and one of the first things I saw when I got over on the main part of town were these little kids. They were over there around a grocery store that was boarded up. Everything had been bombed--I mean, it looked horrible--and these little kids a-standing around there and, of course, they couldn't get in, but that's where they used to get milk, apparently, because this one little kid kept crying, "Our milk, milk, milk." Oh, that gets you. And the others would kind of quiet him, and they'd say nothing, but they just looked around and they had a--well, you can't describe the look on their faces.

But the adults--I never seen people braver or more--I don't know what--had more intestinal stuff in them--I'll tell you--as those people did. We made three liberties over there altogether, counting the other three trips. But we were taken into their homes, and

---

*Henry J. Kaiser (1882-1967) was an American industrialist famous for his feats of ship production in World War II. His shipyards built about one-third of the merchant ships constructed during the war and 50 escort carriers for the Navy--a total of 1,460 ships.

they treated us like family. They would feed us out of their rations and would have been insulted if we hadn't taken it. We would have hurt their feelings. Yet it hurt us to even have to eat it, because they had so little. We had everything we wanted, and it got you.

I know I took this one family over there; I took the old man a bunch of cigars. Oh, did that please him! We sat around. They'd lose a mother or a father and mother, something like that, in bombs and got to where they just gathered together, uncles, aunts and all just in one house, kind of staying close together. But they weren't grieving or anything like that. I mean, they just held up like you can't believe. He'd light up that cigar and he'd sit over there and he'd never say anything. Once in a while you'd hear him say, "Hmph, hmph, Churchill ain't got nothing on me."* [Laughter] That did me a lot of good, seeing him. He'd smoke that thing down to about there--the bitter end. Then he put it the pipe and finished it up in his pipe. [Laughter]

Paul Stillwell: Did you go into any of their pubs?

Mr. Logue: Yes, we did. They had ale, and I sure didn't like the ale. But, you know--this was interesting to me--there was a black man in there, the only one I saw. He was accepted just like everybody else, and he talked with that thick tongue in a Scottish brogue to where you couldn't understand a word he said. I tried. I listened to him, tried my best to converse, but I couldn't tell what he was saying, because they have a thicker tongue or something because he couldn't--now the Scottish--you could understand them pretty well.

Paul Stillwell: I was just wondering, did you have any black sailors in your ship?

Mr. Logue: Yes, oh yes. In fact, in those days the only thing that a black sailor could be was a messman for the officers' quarters. They began to change that toward the last, before I got out, which is a good thing.† They should have done it.

---

*Winston S. Churchill was Prime Minister of the United Kingdom from 1940 to 1945. A cigar in hand was one of his trademarks.
†The Navy began enlisting black sailors for general service ratings--rather than just messman duty--on 1 June 1942.

E. E. Logue (12/13/95) – Page 62

Paul Stillwell: Well, did you mix with them at all?

Mr. Logue: Not much. You'd go through their compartment. They had a compartment of their own--strictly. I'd go through their compartment, especially to fix lights or stuff like that and you'd talk to them. I mean, they had their thing going, and we had ours. That was about it.

Paul Stillwell: Were they treated as warmly as other shipmates?

Mr. Logue: There was a difference. They stayed their place, we stayed ours. That was about the only thing I can really remember about it. I don't think anybody ever treated them bad or anything like that.

Paul Stillwell: But you didn't have the kind of friendships develop that you would with white sailors?

Mr. Logue: No. No, that's true. You didn't. Not then. Not then.

Paul Stillwell: You were talking about you had plenty to eat in the New York. Was she a good feeder?

Mr. Logue: Pretty good, I think, looking back on it. I get meals at home sometimes I wish we hadn't had, but you know what I mean. [Laughter] All in all, I think they did very well. You get used to Navy chow--I did--and you knew what day it was when you saw what the meal was. But, then, outside of that, no, I never had that kind of complaint very much.

Paul Stillwell: Did you go up topside any during these convoy runs and just look out at all those ships?

Mr. Logue: Oh, yes. In fact I had searchlight duty on the mainmast.

Paul Stillwell: Well, tell me about that.

Mr. Logue: Well, you go up there, oh, about dusk. Usually, up there in the North Atlantic that'd be about 8:00 o'clock in the evening, depending on the time of the year. Because up there where we were at I've seen where it was just barely dark for one hour, and then the sun was up again about 1:00 o'clock or 1:30 in the morning.

Paul Stillwell: In the winter it would be just the opposite.

Mr. Logue: Yes, that's right. So, anyhow, but we'd go up there, and my job was not to operate the searchlight; they had searchlight operators for that. My job was to see and replace carbons if necessary and make sure the thing was running. If it pooped out, I had to get it going again right away.

Paul Stillwell: These were the 36-inch searchlights?

Mr. Logue: Yes, sir.

Paul Stillwell: That's a pretty good-size light.

Mr. Logue: Yes, it is. Yes, it's a big one. We had 24s on the forward part of the ship and then on the forward mast area and the 36s just on the mainmast.

Paul Stillwell: What did you use those for?

Mr. Logue: Well, in case the planes came over would be my guess. We didn't use them much. We didn't light them off very much. But one time when we had a terrible fog and we had a cargo ship just right off our port side, we shot our light straight over to him. I couldn't see his, and I don't think they could see ours, but that was the orders. We kept those lights on all during that fog and kept blowing the whistles--all of the ships did, for that matter.

Paul Stillwell: How far away was that ship? A few hundred yards?

Mr. Logue: Oh, more than that. I'd say a quarter of a mile, something like that.

Paul Stillwell: But it was completely blanked off by the fog.

Mr. Logue: Yes. You couldn't see a thing. You couldn't see anything if it had a been 20 yards out there, I don't think. It was dense.

Paul Stillwell: Did you have any trouble with seasickness in the North Atlantic?

Mr. Logue: Well, yes. Not real bad. I was fortunate. I never saw the time when I couldn't eat my supper, and, you know, you got greasy pork chops every time the sea got rough. But I managed it, and most guys, I think, pretty well handled it. And the old ship rolled quite a bit, too, but then--it didn't have the balance that was built into it because they changed it from a coal bunker and some of those compartments didn't have the weight in them that they expected them to have and stuff like that.

Nevertheless, we went across, and I was going to say this one time it was pretty hairy. It was in that same fog. We took the convoy right in until we got in pretty close, and they said there was an air raid coming. We didn't have anything to fight them with. We couldn't find them anyhow, but they couldn't find us either. We could hear their planes, and they circled around and went back because they were running out of fuel, I suppose. Because I understand that they couldn't much more than make their runs on Scotland and then get back. We could hear them, and that was an eerie feeling, I'll tell you for sure. I was out there on the searchlight that night, and don't think I wasn't scared. I was scared. That's all there was to it. I was scared a lot of times, but then that went with it.

Paul Stillwell: Well, would feel fear just during a normal convoy operation?

Mr. Logue: Somewhat. At least to the extent that you knew where you was at. I'll tell you about the first trip over. That was before I got up on the platform. Remember, again, World War I's the only thing we know about a war. My duty in the evening was to stand the watch, and you'd rotate. Some had the 4:00 to 8:00, 8:00 to 12:00, 12:00 to 4:00 and so on, and whatever watch you had. But my watch was on an ammunition hoist, and this would have been for the 5-inch powder cans would come up on the platform. My job would have been--and the crew would have come down and helped me had it been necessary--and we would have transported them over to the next platform, which would have taken them up to the next deck.

Paul Stillwell: Was this a battle station or just a condition watch?

Mr. Logue: Just a condition watch. I guess they wanted to introduce us to the fact that we were at war at that time. But, anyhow, I sat there with earphones on so that they could start those hoists immediately if they had to. Now, these powder cans went to the 5-inch guns, and I never had to do it. But I'd sit there, and over here's the bulkhead, and you didn't dare talk to anybody on those phones or anything else. All you could do was just sit there. And you'd try to think of everything in the world but what you knew what you were going to think about. [Laughter] I'd sit there, and I don't know how many torpedoes I saw coming just on the other side of that bulkhead. Oh, man, I'll tell you. But, finally, you get worn into it, you know.

Paul Stillwell: Where was your battle station?

Mr. Logue: My battle station--boy, oh boy, I got to think on that, on my first one. My battle station later on was the repair party, but where in the world did I go on my first battle station?--I can't--if I can remember it I'll bring it back to you, but I don't remember where I went then for sure.

Paul Stillwell: I wonder if you ever had a sense of claustrophobia when you'd be down inside the ship during general quarters.

Mr. Logue: You know, that's one thing that I never had a lot of trouble with. Oh, you might, you know--but somebody told me years ago when I was working someplace to where I was caught in a real close place, said, "Take quick, short breaths." And I did and it worked. So any time I got to feeling I--huh, huh, huh, huh, huh, huh, huh, huh, huh--like that, you know and kind of wring it out.

I wanted to tell you back over in Scotland on something that impressed me very much.

Paul Stillwell: Okay.

Mr. Logue: We were coming through a park, my buddy John Diamond and myself. We looked at the scenery, and it was pretty and all. Well, we came by and there's quite a few benches along there, and dear old ladies sitting there with their knitting and all. They saw us, and they saw that we were American sailors, and I never was so humiliated in my life. Those ladies got up and bowed to us as we went by--ooooooh. These people had done all the suffering, and then they're up recognizing us in that fashion--so sweet and kind, smiling and all to us. Oh, man!

Then, as we walked along, these little girls, oh, some of them probably young teenagers, would run by and you'd feel them tap you on the back and they'd say something, and I didn't know what it was. Oh, by the way, we had a self-appointed guide that was taking us through there. He was an awful nice young man and we appreciated him. So after they had gone on through, I said, "What in the world did they say and what were they doing? What significance did that have?"

Said, "Well," said, "you know the stars on the back of your collar?"

I said, "Yeah."

Said, "They lick their finger like that, and they jump up and they touch your star and they say 'The best of luck to you, sir'." It was interesting the whole time.

Paul Stillwell: Well, that's the same kind of spirit you encountered in these homes you went into.

Mr. Logue: That's right. That's exactly what I say. I can't think of anything but wonderful things about those people. They were great. I got into a dance hall one night, and I heard them playing a tune that my dad used to play on the fiddle. [Laughter] That tickled me, made me homesick.

Paul Stillwell: I was wondering when you stood these shore patrol duties that you'd mentioned earlier. Was that in the States or overseas or where?

Mr. Logue: Always in the States. I never drew that overseas. If they had them overseas, usually it was a detail that they had over there. It wasn't off the ship. Sometimes it was off the ship.

Paul Stillwell: What did you have to do when you when you were on that duty?

Mr. Logue: Well, you patrolled. You had an area to patrol. There'd be two of you. The main thing that we had to do was clean up the drunks. You tried to get them, but our job was not to get sailors arrested but to keep them out of trouble. And if you could get them away from the police and either get them back to the ship or get them to where they're not causing trouble or anything like that, this was our main job as shore patrol. This was explained to us, and this was what we tried to do, but someone gets so wild sometimes. I know we had one kid one time, and he fought the four guys and we had to take him in--that's all we could do. Policemen followed us to see that we did.

So that went from the better to the worse, and anywhere in between. But that was your job. You were responsible only, of course, for Navy men, and I never bothered anybody much unless they were just--you could see if the police saw him that he'd get him and put him in and you'd try and protect them. Get them away. Get them somewhere to where they could either sleep it off or something so that they wouldn't get put in the jug and get it against them. Because, they got put in the jug, why, he went on report and that went against their record and so forth. So that's mainly what our job was as shore patrol.

Paul Stillwell: I would think getting them back to the ship would be the ideal solution.

Mr. Logue: You can't force them to go back, though, really. You can try to talk them into it and bluff them into it or anything like that, but you're taking a lot on yourself to force them to go back to the ship, because that's their liberty and all. So it was touchy. It wasn't a job I aspired to at all, I'll tell you.

I'll never forget one time. I wasn't on shore patrol then, but I was new and there was this crazy Englishman on our ship. I mean, he was very definitely English descent, but he was an American. I went over with him, and in this bar in Norfolk was a big old U-shaped bar. So we went in there and I'm new now--probably one of the early liberties that I ever took--and I'm learning the ropes. Anyhow, we went through and went around and come back up about halfway on this side, and a beer bottle rolled out across the floor. Came up pretty close to us. This crazy nut turned around, and there wasn't another guy in that room that was off the New York. I was looking around, because the first thing you do is look for buddies in case you do get in trouble.

He was about half drunk, and he turned around and said, "Who threw that?" Boy, oh boy, I mean things got tense in there for a little bit. Finally I eased in behind him and put my arms around his, pinned to his side, started walking, and I said, "Drop that bottle. Whatever you do, drop that bottle easy."

"Oh, I--"

"Shut up and drop that bottle."

He did, so we backed out the door and we got on the outside. I said, "You go your way; I'm going mine. That's it. I got you out of there. That's enough." I thought we were all going get decapitated or something.

Paul Stillwell: Did you have some sea daddies in the ship to kind of teach you the ropes of shipboard life?

Mr. Logue: Yes, I think so. There were those that took an interest in you and helped you. My word, where would we have been without them? I think of them more as an older brother. In a sense, that's the kind of the way I had them, because they didn't mind telling you how silly you were if you were silly, and that's probably a good way to learn too. But, by the same token, they helped you get lined up on the right thing, whether you were doing a job or this ain't the way the Navy does it, even down in the bunkroom or whatever like that, you know, just teaching the ways of the Navy. That was the way the older guys seemed to feel. They felt they were responsible for it, and I think nearly all of them did. Looking back on that, I thought that was a great thing, really.

Paul Stillwell: What examples do you remember of things they taught you?

Mr. Logue: Oh, I suppose I had a tendency to be a blowhard, at least to a degree, and they taught me that that wasn't a nice thing to do. They told me that I didn't know enough to be a blowhard. [Laughter] And, thank God, I listened to them and got by pretty good before it was all over with.

We made those trips in the North Atlantic in '42. We came back in then, and that must have been about sometime in September. Maybe the latter part of September, because for some reason--I was only a third class, but we just had one gyrocompass man. He got to be a chief, and then he had a striker in there and hardly anybody that knew anything about electronics and for some reason--again, I mean, I don't know--I'm not that smart a fellow, but they chose me to go to gyrocompass school in Brooklyn Navy Yard because they thought they ought to have a spare on there anyhow.* That was a four-month school, and they give me 21 days to get from Norfolk to Brooklyn. So I went by way of Wichita, and that's when we got married.

Paul Stillwell: She decided not to wait six years?

---

*The New York Navy Yard was in the borough of Brooklyn. To reach it, ships had to steam up a portion of the East River and go under the Brooklyn Bridge.

Mr. Logue: Well, I pulled it off. I got down there, and she was working at Boeing as a secretary or in a big room of secretaries there, so I went to where I knew she was. She and a girlfriend had an apartment there in Wichita, and I knew right where it was, and I got off the train. I beat it over there and caught her before she went to work. We talked a little bit, and I said, "Now, this is probably the longest time we'll ever have together for as long as this war is going on. How would you like to get married tomorrow?"

She said, "Okay," just like that. She already had the engagement ring, so we went down to the jewelry store and bought the wedding ring. She had to go to work because she worked the evening shift and her ride came by. So she got in there, and I went down to the courthouse and got the marriage license.

I went out to Bentley, to my dad's, and borrowed a '36 Chevy that belonged to Dad's cousin. He was a real dear friend. We were all real close together. He had had a real severe heart attack, and they were pretty hard up. He said, "Ed, I ain't got anything to buy you a wedding present with, but just take this car and use it." I thanked him for that, so we had that.

So then I picked her up, and the guy she was working for was my neighbor buddy out there on the farm. Would you believe it? She didn't know it for sure, and he didn't either for sure till they checked it out. He and I used to go fishing together and everything else, and there he was in charge of all that big office and she was working for him. He says, "You'll be sick today. I'll take care of that." [Laughter]

She just got one day off, so I got a room on the fifth floor of the Allis Hotel, which then was the biggest hotel in Wichita. I could have that for a week, but then Jan Garber and his band was coming in, and it was part of a whole series of rooms--a suite--that the band was taking over, so we had it for five days anyhow. But we went out to Mount Hope then and were married at the parsonage. We were going to do this the simplest and fastest possible and just go to the preacher and get it over with. Her mother had died the same year my mother did. (I never knew hers; she never knew mine.) So there was just her daddy. He was an older fellow, and I was going to have to tell that poor old gentleman that I was going to marry his daughter and taking her away. And she was the last one; she was the youngest. I didn't know how I was going to do that.

So we went out and got her older sister, who was married then and on the farm. She came in with us, and so we went in. I was hemming and hawing around, trying to figure out how to tell him that I was going to marry his daughter. He got to talking about some chickens that he had out there, you know, and so I listened to him. Finally I broke in again and started to say something and nothing to do but go out there with him and see them chickens. So we went out and come back there again and finally, Floy, her sister, whispered in my ear and said, "Do you mind if Daddy went along?"

I said, "I'll be tickled to death to have him." Never even occurred to me, you know. Dumb. But she said, "Well, that might break the ice."

I said, "Well, you want to go down with us if we go down to get married?"

"I'll go right in and get ready," he said. He went in. He called the preacher, lined it all up and everything. And we went down, and we were married there in the preacher's home and took them both home then. We took off and went by Dad's and then went back, and we spent five days there.

Then we had to get out, and we got one other cheaper hotel. This girl that she had an apartment with, her brother was a lawyer there in town, so she moved in with her brother and family. They gave us that apartment then for the rest of the time I was there. So then we figured that was the end of it. Would you believe when I got up there to Brooklyn and got over and got started to school, I saw a bunch of other guys had their wives out there and that the apartments were pretty cheap. You could get some there in Brooklyn, so I called her and asked her how she'd like to come out.

She caught the next plane, and we had four wonderful months in New York City. I mean, we saw all the big bands, we went to all the shows. We saw all the things that you'd go to see--the Statue of Liberty and the Wall Street, even. I'd heard of Wall Street all my life, so we went down to Wall Street. Up on top of the Empire State Building.

I've got to tell you about New Year's Eve there. We laugh about this yet. I had a little buddy there in the school named Shorty Watson, and he was a little short guy. Have you ever seen New York City on New Year's Eve?

Paul Stillwell: I've seen it on television.

Mr. Logue: Mister, I'm telling you, that whole area is full, and they've got policemen lined up with their hands like that--everybody goes this way over here and they go--and nobody tries to go back the other way. Why they'd tromp on you. So here we go. There's Mickey and I and Shorty and Jewell, people on this side of me and on this side. We're just side by side, moving along as we go, and they're playing the music up there and one thing and another. Well, here's this poor drunk down there at the end of the sidewalk, right in the street part there and he's having the time of his life. Every time they come along there he sizes up the lady and he grabs her, hugs her, kisses her, and sets her down. Everybody's having' a big time, so what, you know. And in a while he goes back and gets the next one.

Well, we're going along there like I said, Mickey's right in line. I thought, "Well, this might be fun. That little old Kansas girl--I don't know how she'll take that, but it's something that might be funny." So just as we got there I give a lunge to the side and he grabbed Shorty. Picked him up--he was about to kiss old Shorty. [Laughter] I'm telling you, that was the funniest thing. Old Shorty's eyes got that big--I think it sobered the drunk. Oh, man, I'll tell you we had a time over that. But we did have a lot of fun in New York.

Paul Stillwell: Did your wife's boss hold her job for her?

Mr. Logue: Well, no, but she went right back, and they took her on again. But she was there four months and in the meantime--during those four months--Scotty Umsted took that ship down to Casablanca. Well, he had to go to Safi with the <u>New York</u>, and I guess they had quite a deal over there.* He blew them out of the water and they conquered Safi. But they had another battleship and several heavy cruisers and lots of--

Paul Stillwell: <u>Massachusetts</u> was over there at Casablanca, I know.

---

*As part of the Allied invasion of French Morocco, U.S. troops landed at Safi on 8 November 1942. The <u>New York</u> was credited with neutralizing the formidable Batterie Bailleuse, the strongest coastal defense unit in the region.

Mr. Logue: Okay. And several others and I guess they were holding them out there. They said this Jean Bart was in port there.* And the only turret she had active they tell me they got--all I know is what they told me when they come back--but said it was the rear turret. But they said he had about a 20- to a 22-mile range and said he was holding them out, and so here comes old Scotty over there. Now, this is what they told me--that old Scotty passed the word, "We can't fight them at that range. Let's go in and fight them at ours." And I guess they laid up an antiaircraft barrage, and old New York started in and, you know, they got about halfway in and the white flag went up on the Jean Bart. Now, the only thing they could figure was that they saw, "Hey, here's another battleship. What's the use?" They could have blown us out of the water, but they didn't.

Paul Stillwell: Did you feel a sense of disappointment in missing out on the Casablanca operation with your shipmates?

Mr. Logue: In a sense, yes, and one of the reasons for that I can only guess, but the last trip to Casablanca, when they came back up again--this is just what they told me--we had steam steering and electric steering on that ship. And normally you're supposed to hold your steam steering for auxiliary and use your electrical, but instead they did opposite. They went the other way and always used it. I don't know why. That was the fault of the engineering department. But, anyhow, the thing went haywire on them. They were the leader, and they pretty near hit every ship in the convoy to get to the rear, because they lost their control. They finally got to the back and got straightened out enough to where they could bring it in, but they never had much faith on that old tub after that.

Paul Stillwell: When did this happen?

Mr. Logue: Just before they went over.

Paul Stillwell: Were you still on board at the time?

---

*On 10 November 1942, during the invasion of Casablanca, French Morocco, the New York was only 5,000 yards from the USS Augusta (CA-31) when the heavy cruiser was bombarded by the incomplete French battleship Jean Bart, which was immobilized in Casablanca Harbor.

Mr. Logue: No, no, I was still in school.

Paul Stillwell: All right.

Mr. Logue: I'm still in school. That's why I say this is what they told me when they came in. So when I came in and my school was over--incidentally, a chief petty officer who had just had the fit when they sent me to school, anyhow, because, "They could send somebody else. I can use that guy," or something like that. He was carrying on about it. But I went over, and the next thing I know, they're in the big naval building, where all the offices and everything were in Brooklyn. It's across the road and down from the yard. I saw old Billy Simpson in there. I said, "What in the world are you doing in here"

"Ha, ha, ha," he said. "You're aren't the only one that can get off that ship."

Paul Stillwell: Who was he?

Mr. Logue: He was the chief petty officer in the light shop and the one I worked for in there and learned an awful lot from. And I was still third class. But he was going to take a new destroyer out, and he wanted me to get on that new destroyer with him. He said, "I'd love to have somebody on there I know in the shop," I had never been on a destroyer much and all, but I finally agreed because they could get me, that is, if I graduated before that ship went into commission. They could get me if I would agree to go, is the way the Navy had it set up at that time, and so I said, "Okay."

So I never thought much more about it until it came time for graduation, and he came over there. They were getting ready to put it in commission. He said, "When you going to graduate?" And I give him the date. "Oh, oh," he said. "We're going to miss it one day and we can't get you." Hey, listen. They took that ship out and sunk it the very first time. All hands."

Paul Stillwell: What ship was it?

Mr. Logue: I can't remember the name of it now. It was a brand-new destroyer. Went out into the Atlantic and she got sunk and lost all hands, Biffy and the whole works. That was all I really knew about it, but you talk about a close call--one day.

Paul Stillwell: So you really felt a sense of loyalty to the New York after that.

Mr. Logue: Oh, boy. But, I mean Biffy was a friend--that was a terrible thing.

Paul Stillwell: Please tell me about the course work at the gyro school. How did that go?

Mr. Logue: Oh. We had mostly class work.

Paul Stillwell: Where was it held? In the navy yard?

Mr. Logue: Yes, in the navy yard, in a special room that they had in there. They had some intelligent instructors, and I want you to know it. Those men knew their stuff, and they were good. I mean, none of this old Navy stuff. We were in a classroom, and these were instructors.

Paul Stillwell: Were they from the Sperry Company?

Mr. Logue: No. No. They were naval people. But they were definitely instructors, and they were good. I felt like we learned a lot. I was real pleased about it. I said we had four months. It must have been three months, because I had a month of daylight and I had a month of evening classes and a month of daylight again. That's the way it was. They switched back and forth.

Paul Stillwell: Why did they do that? Do you know?

Mr. Logue: No, I don't unless it was because they had other classes.

Paul Stillwell: I see. They were running in shifts.

Mr. Logue: Yes.

Paul Stillwell: Well, that makes sense.

Mr. Logue: Yes. So then when we finished there, why, I sent Mickey back to Kansas. The Navy sent me over to Pier 92, and that was a hell hole. Had you ever heard about that?

Paul Stillwell: No.

Mr. Logue: Oh. Captain's wife would come down there and put you on report. If she was walking through there and you weren't doing just to suit her, why, she'd call some patrol over there and say, "Put this man on report." That's the only time in my life I ever saw a four-striper come around and beat on bunks and hold reveille.

Paul Stillwell: Did they put you in a ship there?

Mr. Logue: No, it was a receiving station. Pier 92 was a receiving station, but it was a hell hole.

Paul Stillwell: They had kind of a barracks on the pier?

Mr. Logue: Yes, yes. They had it up there. It was two stories, and we had barracks up above on this top story, where we had our bunks anyhow.

Paul Stillwell: I heard there was one of those coal-burning ships, I think a cruiser there, that supplied the power, wasn't there?

Mr. Logue: Might have been. Now, I couldn't say that for sure. I got out of there as fast as I could. Quick as my ship come in, boy, I was over there on it. So those guys went over to France. All we did just kind of patrol there for a while till finally they found something we could do. They were getting these destroyer escorts lined up and the crews for them. They were sending their gunnery crews over to the New York, and we would take them out for a week of gunnery training.

Paul Stillwell: What kind of guns were these?

Mr. Logue: We had 3-inch, and I imagine that's what they were working on and 20 millimeters, would be my guess. Now, of course, again I'm down below decks and didn't pay that much attention, but I knew they were on there for gunnery training, and we did that now for months.

Paul Stillwell: This would be year '43.

Mr. Logue: Yes. Nearly the whole year after I went down there. Let's see, I went to school in November, December, January, and then probably by March or April I would have been on back on the New York again. We went down around Norfolk and operated out of Norfolk. We'd stay out a week and come in over weekends and get liberty, whatever we rated. I brought Mickey back down to Norfolk then. She even went to work in the naval ammunition depot in an office down there then. So she was there from '43 clear over till December of '44 when we went through the ditch.*

Paul Stillwell: Did you feel any sense of envy of these men who'd been through the North Africa operation?

Mr. Logue: No, no, no. I didn't have anything like that, other than the fact that I felt bad that we couldn't have been there. I felt like the old New York deserved that and--I don't

---

*The New York left for the West Coast on 21 November, transited the Panama Canal, and arrived at San Pedro, California, on 6 December 1944.

know that the reason I gave you was the reason they didn't take her. They'd have to leave one ship back there at least, as well as some cruisers, so I don't know what the reason was they didn't take her.

I've got to tell you about the battery now. This is where it comes in. I was boat and battery electrician for probably a year and a half anyhow, and, for all small boats and everything. See, that ship's alternate power was great, big old six-volt storage batteries, linked together, of course. And I had my panel in there and everything for them. I had to keep them charged, and every six months, why, you cycled them, so on and so forth. Also, I had to have batteries for the gun mounts up on the air castle there and also had to have batteries for all the boats.

Well, the old man had about a '37 or '38 Lincoln. He wanted to buy a battery, but it was during the war, and he wasn't eligible to buy a battery, so therefore he was trying to make out the best way he could, I guess, and I can't hardly blame him for that.

Paul Stillwell: Apparently whoever was controlling batteries figured he would be at sea and didn't really need his car.

Mr. Logue: That's probably very likely, but it just didn't work out.

Paul Stillwell: Was this Captain Umsted?

Mr. Logue: No, no, no. This was M. C. Christian. Umsted left and went to other things to do after the Casablanca deal, and so here we got Christian. He was in there with that, and he called me up there one day. "Sparky," he said, "you got any batteries down there?"

I said, "Yes, sir. We've got a lot of batteries down there."

"You got one that would fit my Lincoln?"

I said, "Well, Captain, I imagine I'd have to say no, but I will go measure if you like, and I'll see what you have and see what can be done."

"You do that, Sparky."

So I did, and just like I thought and knew, your automobile battery was much shorter, squattier. All I had to be compared to it was these batteries that was going up to the gun mounts. Now, you probably understand storage batteries very well, but your automobile has very thin plates and a lot of them to give a quick surge of power. You've got a lot more power. But these for the gun batteries--they wanted them to last for a long time, and they don't need a surge of power, so they're thick plates and not near as many.

In the first place, I couldn't believe that there'd be enough sudden power there to even turn that thing over with those batteries, but the thing on top of that was that they were too tall. They wouldn't fit underneath the seat. So then they said, "Well can't you get some of them boat batteries and put them under there?"

"Where you going to put it? Under the seat?"

"Well, no." Now, these are some of the other officers talking to me like this. Sparky O, we'll call him. That's what everybody else did. He was a warrant officer, and his name was Oliver.[*] He was trying to make points with that captain in the worst way, and he didn't know the first thing about batteries or even electricity. How he ever got to be a warrant officer--well, there's only one other way.

Paul Stillwell: Not exactly legal, is it either, to use a government battery in this man's car?

Mr. Logue: No, but I mean who was going to tell the captain? Not me. Captain says do that, I'm going to do it. Let him answer the consequences. It's his car they're going to catch it in. So, no, it wasn't legal, but then nevertheless that was what was coming off, and old Sparky O was trying to make his points.

I kept telling him, I said, "Mr. Oliver, that's not going to fit in there."

"Well, why can't you use a boat battery?"

"Well," I said, "look how big they are. How you going to get it underneath the seat in the first place?"

"Well, can't you put it in the trunk?"

I said, "Yeah, where you going to get battery cables long enough to reach from the trunk clear up to the generator of your car and so forth?"

"Well, couldn't you make any?"

I said, "You got any place down here to make them with?"

---

[*]Electrician George A. Oliver, USN.

"No." By then he'd been talked out of it, I think. I had to go up and keep charging, get his battery out and keep bringing it down and charging it for him. I got some late liberties on the deal, too, because I couldn't leave without his battery charged up enough to where he could get back the next day.

Paul Stillwell: Was this the car's regular battery?

Mr. Logue: Yes.

Paul Stillwell: Okay.

Mr. Logue: So then old Sparky O come down there one day, and he had it all figured out. I don't know what he thought he knew, but he said, "Logue, come here. Get that battery and let's go."

"Okay, Mr. Oliver." I took one of those little gun mount batteries, and we went up there. We took the seat out and we took the battery out that was in there. "Sure enough, it was a lot shorter, Mr. Oliver."

"You just do as I say. Just put her in there."

"All right, sir." So I put it in, and I hooked her up and we set it in there.

"Now," he said, "we'll try it." So he got in there, wiggling his butt around in the seat a little bit, and tried to turn the switch, and he just got a grunt. About that time the smoke come pouring out around that seat up there. He jumped out of there. We grabbed that seat and pulled it out--big old hole burned in the burlap of that thing, right where the captain sat. Oh, man. And poor old Sparky was running out there [unclear]. There'd been a snow and big piles of it there--running up banging snow over in his hands trying to put some of the [unclear] that was still smoking. I couldn't do anything but just sit there grit my teeth. If I laughed, and I knew I'd laugh, I would be in trouble. So after they got settled down, why, he said, "Well, you go in and tell the captain what happened." Me go in and tell the captain.

Paul Stillwell: That was real nice of him.

Mr. Logue: Yes. Well, I knew that's what was coming, and I was getting pretty well acquainted with him. He wasn't a bad old guy, especially if he wanted something, so I went up and told the Marine who I was and to see the captain. He heard my name and said, "Come on in, Logue."

So I walked in and I said, "Yes, sir."

Well, he said, "How did it work?" So I knew the captain and Oliver was in on the deal together, or he wouldn't ask.

I said, "Captain, it didn't work very well."

He turned around. "What's the matter?"

"Well," I said, "I believe I made the statement that was too tall for that quite some time ago, and I wasn't wrong." I said, "When we put it in there and it didn't have enough power to turn it over, but it had power enough to burn a hole in the burlap underneath your seat."

I was just waiting until he exploded. He sat there a little bit, turned around. Pretty soon he turned around to his desk and put his back behind me. I swear I saw his shoulders shake a little bit like he might have been laughing or something. I just stood there, and pretty soon he said, kind of out of the side of his mouth, "Was Mr. Oliver scared?"

I said, "Yes, sir, and so was I."

"That'll be all, Sparky." (Sparky was what he called me.) I left and that was all I ever heard of batteries for his car. I never heard another word, boy. Okay.

Paul Stillwell: So it was up to Oliver to fix it then?

Mr. Logue: Well, yes. He could have arranged whatever he wanted, but they didn't go through me. Nothing happened, though, because I did have to keep charging his battery.

But we were out to sea--quite a bit of patrolling and then this DE student training that I spoke about. This went on for months.

Paul Stillwell: Sounds like there wasn't a real job for the New York.

Mr. Logue: There wasn't. We were just patrolling. We would patrol while they did this.

Paul Stillwell: No more convoys, though.

Mr. Logue: No. The most boring thing that we had--we'd had nothing--you might say through the winter of '43 and '44--the first part of '44. Then we took the midshipmen on three different cruises in the summer of '44.

Paul Stillwell: Where did you go?

Mr. Logue: Oh, I can't think of the island, but we went over in the West Indies and messed around there for a week or two. Would you believe I gave 12 lectures a day?

Paul Stillwell: On what?

Mr. Logue: Well, sir, I gave about a 15- to 20-minute lecture on emergency power. I gave a 20-minute lecture on distribution, from the distribution boards and all that, and 20 minutes on gyrocompass. They were all right there together, see? One here, one here and one here and as far as [unclear] was concerned I was qualified in all of them. By that time I think I was second class and so--but I did that to--let's see, four classes. And, you know, some of those guys couldn't get as much as they needed, and those guys would come around after supper with their books and all and ask if they could have help. I said, "Well, shoot, yeah."

Paul Stillwell: That's impressive.

Mr. Logue: So they came down, and they'd shoot their questions, and I'd give them the best I could on it, you know. So I was real pleased that they were interested that much in it.

Paul Stillwell: Sure.

Mr. Logue: But mainly just patrolling and all. Like I said, it was very boring clear on up till--

Paul Stillwell: Had the ship gone in the yard again after she got fixed from that grounding?

Mr. Logue: Yes. We spent some time in the yard. I don't remember for sure just what period of time.

Paul Stillwell: I think you said at some point they converted from hammocks to bunks.

Mr. Logue: Oh, that was way back in the beginning.

Paul Stillwell: I see.

Mr. Logue: Yes, that was clear back when I first went aboard. We were on hammocks for a very short time on the deck. And then soon they got things straightened out and built more bunks and all, and we all got bunks. In fact, they eventually took our hammocks away from us.

Paul Stillwell: Did you say also that they set up a general mess in place of these division messes you'd had?

Mr. Logue: Yes, I'm going to say probably in '44, why, they came in and had them put in the cafeteria style. That's right. And we all ate on the second deck from then on.

Paul Stillwell: Which did you prefer?

Mr. Logue: The cafeteria.

Paul Stillwell: Why?

Mr. Logue: Well, you went through the line yourself that way and had a little more choice of what you wanted. When you got through, all you did was take your tray and dump it all and get rid of it. You didn't have mess cooks to fool with, taking tables down, and so forth. I don't know, it just seemed more efficient or something, and I think I enjoyed it better.

Paul Stillwell: I would think that you would not have as much fellowship, though, being with the same guys at your meals.

Mr. Logue: This is true but then, well, what do you call fellowship? You got the first class down here at the head, and he is the head, and the second class is number two heads and on down. I don't know, about all they did was ride the under guys.

Paul Stillwell: So you would find it desirable to get away from that.

Mr. Logue: I did. However, by the time we had it, I was one of the upper guys myself. But I never did appreciate the way they were doing it, and I never did do it that way. I tried to be helpful to the guys, because that kind of bothered me a little when I was in there. Maybe it shouldn't have, but it did.

Paul Stillwell: Well, I got the impression, too, that the senior men at the table liked to take the better food too: the biggest piece of meat and so forth.

Mr. Logue: They were taking food; you're right there. It went to the head, and then the guys according to rank or rate, they were, on down here, and you got what was left when the plate got down to you. That's true.

Paul Stillwell: Was there gambling on board the New York?

Mr. Logue: Ha, ha, ha. You've got to be kidding, aren't you?

Paul Stillwell: I'm asking.

Mr. Logue: Yes, indeed. Yes, indeed. There was. In fact, they got a big poker game. When I made first class in '44, I had charge of the light shop then. Don Zarr was the chief, and he went down to chiefs' quarters.* Poor Don hadn't been on there very long, anyhow, so he just left it all to me. I grew up on the thing and all. But he was nice. He was a good chief and we got along real good. I'm sorry. Where was I?

Paul Stillwell: Gambling.

Mr. Logue: Yes. This one guy was quite a rounder anyhow and quite a gambler. He got a whole bunch of them down there on the distribution board just outside the light shop. Well, technically that was my area of responsibility. I let it go on for about three or four nights. Finally I come out and I said, "Hey, this is no Reno, Nevada. Out with this. I'm not going to be the one that's going to get it if they come down and catch you." And, oh, I thought this guy was going to whip me.

I said, "Well, you may be able to whip me, but it isn't going to alter a thing. You're getting out of here with this. I'm not having it down here. Now, if you want me to bring somebody down here to move you out, I can do it." They moved out so, okay, that's all there is to it. That ended the gambling in my area. But, hey, that's dangerous, you know. They can get pretty vicious on that, some of those guys. If the wrong officer would have come down there and caught them, why, he'd have come right to me because that was the area I was responsible for. So we didn't have much right there, but there was a lot of different corners on the ship.

Now, some of the guys played it pretty cool. If they won, they could go up to the post office and make out a money order and send it home. And if they didn't, they didn't have that much to lose so they were making money. And other of them poor suckers, why, if they won it they went back and lost it the next day and all. I felt sorry for them in a way,

---

*Chief Electrician's Mate Don Wayne Zarr, USN.

and I didn't in another way. But that was about all I knew about gambling. We got them out of down there.

Paul Stillwell: What sort of things did you do for recreation in off hours? Have movies?

Mr. Logue: When we weren't in any area, we had movies every night on the forecastle, usually.

I'll tell you, probably one of the most dangerous jobs that we had that I got into--and this was before I made first class--was the fighting lights. Now, they were an extension of the foremast, and it was a yardarm that went out that way. There was a metal box about that tall and about that wide.

Paul Stillwell: About six inches wide and a foot tall maybe?

Mr. Logue: Maybe five inches--six sounds big. Those lights had different colors. I've forgotten what they were now, but when you flashed your fighting lights--as you probably know that was to let any ships in the area that you were under attack and that you were fighting. I don't know that we ever used it.

Paul Stillwell: Well, I think the idea was for recognition, so you could tell friend from foe in the dark.

Mr. Logue: Oh, is that it? I'll bet you're right on that then. You're right. Because I never did know for sure what it was about. All I know is that to get up there you had to straddle that yardarm, and you went way out past the edge of the ship. And then to work on that thing you locked this leg and this arm and come clear around and reached around and hung there while that thing was doing this.

Paul Stillwell: Did you have a safety belt?

Mr. Logue: No. What good would it have done? We'd have just laid there and hung. And you took your bulbs out and you changed them or anything you had to do on it. And you came back in. Now, let's see. When we were coming into port, at a certain point we had to go up and take the bulbs out of those lights so they couldn't in no way that they could come on. Then after we passed a certain point, going back out to sea again, we had to go up and put them back in.

I had another nasty job. I don't know why the Navy did things like this, but they tied these motor launches to a boat boom on the after part of the ship that stuck out there. Then they got a little old rope ladder down, and they put it down just about far enough to where you had to go down with your hands and then drop into the boat, instead of putting down where you could just step away from it.

Well now, those batteries that went into the boat must have weighed from 60 to 80 pounds and a boat when the batteries go bad and you have to change them, why, the only way I could do it was to bring that thing up three flights of stairs--you would call them; it would be the same equivalent--carry it across the deck from the forecastle clear back to the after part of the ship, say, turret number four, and there's your boat boom going out there, and that boat's tied up there.

Then you've got to take a rope and you straddle that. Now, you've got four batteries to change and those jewels, like I say, they weigh around at least 80 pounds. You're sliding back and pulling that battery with you after you've already got a rope tied on it and tied to the boom. Then you let that thing down, and then your boat's doing this and this and this so--

Paul Stillwell: Rocking back and forth.

Mr. Logue: Right, and you've got to wait until you get it down as close to them devils as you can and as quick as you can get them down.

Paul Stillwell: Was there somebody at the bottom to catch it?

Mr. Logue: No. There wasn't anybody to help you. That was my job. So you drop it down in there. Then you jump down into that from the end of the rope ladder, and take the old one off. Now, here's where the fun comes in. You tie it on to the old one, put the new one in, get up, pull that thing up on to that boom, and take it back. You do that four times. And if you think that isn't half a day's work, try it.

Paul Stillwell: How high off the water were those yardarms that you had to go out and change the bulbs?

Mr. Logue: Oh, my word. Well, they were clear up--long ways up. I--

Paul Stillwell: Seventy-five, eighty feet?

Mr. Logue: How far would the bridge be up?

Paul Stillwell: I don't know.

Mr. Logue: Well, I bet it was, because we were up higher than the bridge and--then, of course, you got the part of the ship that's out of the water between--I don't know. I just never thought of it, I guess. It just looked a long ways on it from up there. It wasn't my favorite game at all.

Paul Stillwell: What was the relationship between the officers and enlisted men in that ship?

Mr. Logue: I imagine about like it would be anywhere. Some of them were real great guys, some of them were average, and some of them were stinkers. And I think the enlisted men were the same way. They just were people. The way I think of it anyhow is that we had some fine officers that I really appreciated. We had some that I thought were stinkos, and probably some of them thought I was a stinko, and maybe I was. I don't know.

Paul Stillwell: There probably wasn't a lot of fraternization. You didn't shoot the breeze with them.

Mr. Logue: Not much. Not much. Now, we had a little warrant officer name of Everetts. At one time I was in charge of the storeroom down there where all the parts and everything were. He was always coming down and drinking coffee and visiting with me. He was a warrant officer, and he was a nice guy. So there was a few of them. I liked him, and Mr. Simpson was a nice guy. He was the one that came right after Sparky O. They got rid of him finally.

I wish I could give you a better answer than that, but in thinking back I can't remember an officer that I hated. I remember some that I used to get disgusted with, and I'm sure they did me. I remember most of them, though, that I had anything to do with were good men, and I thought that under the circumstances they did as good a job as they could and I was trying to do the same thing. So I don't remember anything bad really about anyone.

Paul Stillwell: How much association did you have with the Marines?

Mr. Logue: I had a Marine buddy. That was fun too. Max Lloyd. He was a sergeant, and he was next to the top sergeant, whatever that was. At that time I was first class. His wife and my wife worked at the same place, and they would see each other at the deal. Well, they were a kind of a couple, and they were good kids. We run around with them on the beach on liberty and all, but they were the kind that liked to be just a step ahead of everybody and everything. They wanted to know a little more than anybody else--they wanted to be the first to this and that and the other thing--and it didn't bother us any. Didn't make any difference anyhow, so that didn't interfere with our relationship.

But when we'd go out, like on those cruises with the DE students, we'd come in on the weekend. Or even we'd be gone several weeks with the midshipmen and then come back in, why, I'd get on the phone. At that time the E division had the telephone up there, and it was just right straight above a ladder up where the light shop was. There was the light shop and the forward board and a ladder right up to the central station, which is where the telephone was.

So I'd just call in there to the guy, who would plug me in. I'd call over there to the ammunition depot. I called it, and I talked to Mickey a little bit, told her we were in, and I'd probably be over either tonight or tomorrow night. Well, then old Max would rush down there and get the telephone and his wife would chew him out. "How come Ed was able to call our there before you did? How come you couldn't? You're a marine. You ought to be able to--" This and that.

He'd come down there and chew me out. "Don't tell me your troubles." So, finally, they changed around; they did this every once in a while. We had electrician striker who did the telephone operator work, so they took ours off, and they put Marines on there. So we went out on that cruise, and we couldn't get ashore, but the ship's band could. I had a buddy on the ship's band--and wherever it was over there, you could get this French perfume that was real nice. You could get it for, I think, $5.00 a bottle. In the States it cost about $40.00 or $50.00.

Paul Stillwell: This is in the Caribbean.

Mr. Logue: Yes. So I gave this guy $10.00, and I said, "Get me a couple of bottles of the best there, and I'll just take it to my wife. That'll surprise her." So I never even thought anything about it. So we went back in, pulled into port, and we stopped there. I was just moseying around. I wasn't even going to try to phone. I didn't have a chance. See, his man was on board. He'd already told him, "Don't you put a phone call through for Logue till I get mine through." And that guy was scared of his Marine sergeant. Of course, he was going to do it that way. I didn't care and Mickey didn't care. She just laughed about it.

So we pulled in there, and we didn't tie up. And I was standing there trying to catch on. We had the cargo net and some of the guys was getting ready to go over on that cargo net. I got a brilliant idea right quick. I thought, "I'll have me some fun out of this. I don't think we're going to stay here." So I ran down into the light shop right quick, and I got me a tool or two and jumped on that cargo net just as it was leaving. The officer of the deck ran up, and he said, "Where you going?"

I said, "I'm going over to look at the ship's car and truck over there that we have to check."

"Okay. Okay." [Laughter] So I went over and they set me down. Then I went right over to the Marine barracks and called Mickey. They took that ship out, and it took them about three or four hours later before they got it docked. My Marine buddy went up there, and he was going to be number one. When he talked to his wife, she was right in the middle of him: "Ed called her three hours ago. How did he do that?" So I was ornery--I know it--but I couldn't resist it. So about that time I went down and was coming aboard, and who was standing on the quarterdeck waiting for me?

Paul Stillwell: Must have been the Marine.

Mr. Logue: What made it worse, too, was I sent that perfume over, and the next day she took that to work with her and Edna Fay saw that and, of course, Max didn't bring her any. Oh, that was sneaking stuff, but we had fun.

Paul Stillwell: Sounds like it. What were the heads like in a ship that was built before World War I?

Mr. Logue: Troughs with seats that came down on them, and that's all these ever had that I know of.

Paul Stillwell: Did you have that business of just getting a bucket of water a day and having to use that?

Mr. Logue: Yes. That's right. Down in the tropics. When you were up in cooler weather, why, it wasn't so necessary. Of course, they had to use the evaporators, and they would overwork them, so you'd have to take a bucket of fresh water and go up and take your shower in salt water. Then you'd come back and you did your clothes and shaved with your fresh water. And that was it.

We went over the equator, and I got to be a shellback, bless my little heart.

Paul Stillwell: When was that?

Mr. Logue: Okay, that was after we went across. In December '44 we went through the canal, around to San Diego, and then to Hawaii.

Paul Stillwell: I think the Texas and Missouri went out about that same time.

Mr. Logue: Same time. We were going over because Iwo Jima was coming up.[*] And so we then all headed for Kwajalein.[†]

Paul Stillwell: Did you spend any time in Hawaii?

Mr. Logue: Some. We had some liberty over there.

Paul Stillwell: What was that like?

Mr. Logue: Well, of course now, this was several years after the attack. Because it was December when we went out, so it's either the very end of '44 or the beginning of '45. I couldn't say for sure that. We went from the port there at Hawaii to Kwajalein. And just before we got to Kwajalein--now, that's where we threw a blade on one of those propellers. They had three blades on the props, and as I told you with the two engines you just had the two shafts going out. And there was three blades on each prop.

---

[*]On 19 February 1945, U.S. Marines invaded the island of Iwo Jima, approximately 660 miles south of Tokyo, and captured it in a fierce campaign. The objective was to provide a forward airfield--an emergency landing site--to support the U.S. bomber offensive against Japan.

[†]U.S. troops had invaded Kwajalein Atoll in the western Marshall Islands on 1 February 1944. Kwajalein fell on 6 February, and the entire atoll was declared secured. It subsequently served as a base for U.S. warships as the Central Pacific offensive moved closer to Japan.

Okay. You know what that did to that with only two left and clear off center. So they eased us up. They sent a diver down in Kwajalein, and, sure enough, he confirmed what we had. The admiral told us to go back for repairs, but our skipper begged to go along on the operation. He said, "Let me go along and use up some of my ammunition anyhow." Because we had to bombard Iwo before they could land, so we went in and we bombarded until we had them landed.

Paul Stillwell: What do you remember about that battle? Where were you?

Mr. Logue: Well, I was in my place down below, right where I always was, in the repair party. I had the responsibility if anything happened.

Paul Stillwell: Were you the team leader.

Mr. Logue: Well, yes. What you call, I guess, the one responsible for the party. There was four of us, and we had the after gyro, the after fireroom, and the carpenter shop. We had that whole section down there--the whole works in there for anything that went out electrically, where we could get down there and get repaired if possible. Tommy Gregg had it on the starboard side, and I had it on the port.

Anyhow, we were there during that and also during Okinawa, but Iwo Jima, we weren't there very long.* We were there until we landed them, and then we stayed about two days after that to pick off all we could. We took aboard about eight or ten critically injured men. We had to bury three of them at sea. We had three rooms that could be used as operating rooms.

I wonder where some of the younger officers got their education, because I mean those doctors are working frantically now, right around the corner, right through one bulkhead, which, of course, was sealed for watertight protection. Well, right around there and then another bulkhead into a compartment--that's where he was operating. He was that

---

*U.S. forces invaded the island of Okinawa, only 340 miles from the closest point in the Japanese home islands, on 1 April 1945.

close to me. So he called out there to me and said, "Can't we get some air in here? We're trying to operate on this man to save his life. Can't we get some air in here?"

I said, "Well, Doc, hang on just a minute. I'll do what I can." So I called the forward board and got ahold of my division officer. Well, he was one of these guys that gives me the impression that he was a civilian too long and an officer too short, and just because he had friends--no, I won't say that--but, anyhow, he never was an adequate--in my opinion, I'll say now, a far as--I got along, but then he took a little work sometimes.

Paul Stillwell: He was a disappointing man.

Mr. Logue: Well, it was the lack of qualification that bothered me. I have to say that because he just absolutely wasn't qualified for his job.

Paul Stillwell: What was his reaction to this request?

Mr. Logue: "Why, no. You know better than that, Logue. There is no way about it."
I said, "Wouldn't you call the bridge and check."
"Absolutely not. I'm running this down here at this end."
"All right, sir."
So I went back to the doctor on the phone and told him.
He said, "Hang loose."
It wasn't long till I got a call again: "Logue, you better go over there and open that vent up so they can get a little air." The captain had told him differently.

Paul Stillwell: The captain told your division officer?

Mr. Logue: Yes. I heard that the doctor called the bridge and told him, "I'm trying to save a man's life. I need some air down here, and I can't get it, and the forward distribution board refuses to cut in the switch." And he told him, "I'm cutting in the switch. You go ahead and hook it up." I did, so we had air for him.

Paul Stillwell: Did you go topside at all during the bombardment?

Mr. Logue: Yes, I did, one time.

Paul Stillwell: What could you see?

Mr. Logue: I didn't see a lot. This was over at Okinawa, and at that time you laid low until they give you a target, and then you'd pull in and sight in that target and start firing. And, yes, we were firing that time, because the pilot had just come in and said his generator had just gone out on his airplane. I thought I saw him start that thing with a cartridge one time, so I'm scratching my head here, thinking maybe somebody wanted a cup of coffee or something. But, anyhow, they sent me up because they put all the aviation mechs on the beach over there, and there wasn't anybody else. I didn't know anything about an airplane, but I was the only one on the ship that had ever had anything to do with batteries and starter motors and generators and things like that.

So my brilliant division officer said, "Logue, go up and fix the generator on that." Just like that, see. So you obey orders. So I went up topside, and I mean we had planes in the air and we had some firing going off on the beach. This is Okinawa again. So I crawled up. It was on top of turret number three; that's where part of the catapult was, where they hooked it up there.* So I went up there, and the first place I went to was the dashboard, trying to find an ammeter. If he's got a generator, he's got an ammeter. But, no ammeter.

So then I took my time, and I mean it was lonesome up there, I'm telling you. Well, that stuff was booming around you, and I wanted down off of there. Even the guys in the air castle was hiding out, which I don't blame them. They couldn't use them at that time, but I stayed there long enough, and I looked over everything. I didn't want to be caught short and somebody say, "Well, we found it. How come you couldn't find the generator?" So I stayed with that jewel until I had gone over every bit of that electrical

---

*During World War II battleships and cruisers carried floatplanes that were launched from catapults and recovered by cranes. The planes were used for spotting the fall of gunfire so they could give corrections to be used in aiming subsequent rounds.

outfit there. So I think to myself, "Now, I've been the Navy long enough to learn a few things." So I went down and reported in.

The division officer said, "Did you get it fixed?"

I said, "She's ready to go." I never heard another word about it. Never a word.

Paul Stillwell: I think you're right about that pilot wanting some coffee.

Mr. Logue: I do too. I always did believe it.

Paul Stillwell: Could you see the shells landing on the beach?

Mr. Logue: No. No. They were shooting those jewels over several miles and over the top of a hill.

Paul Stillwell: Was any fire coming out in your direction?

Mr. Logue: No, just the airplanes.

Paul Stillwell: But you were apprehensive anyway.

Mr. Logue: Yes, they were dropping some stuff from the planes around there, trying to hit some of the smaller ships.

Paul Stillwell: I see.

Mr. Logue: But, they didn't hit us, just made a lot of noise.

Paul Stillwell: What happened about the ship's damaged propeller?

Mr. Logue: Oh. They sent us back then after they got us out. We went up to the Admiralty Islands.

Paul Stillwell: Was this after Iwo and before Okinawa?

Mr. Logue: Yes.

Paul Stillwell: Did you go to Manus?

Mr. Logue: That's where we went. Absolutely. Manus is in the Admiralty Islands and to a floating dry dock. We were up out of the water, with that heat up there on the equator on the sides of that ship, for 30 days. By the time we got up there, we knocked one off of the other side and we were going up there. About four or five knots was our top speed. So when we got in there, why, they had to make us props for that thing and fly them out to us. And they finally got out there, and by the time we got them on it was the 30 days. When they started Okinawa, we were there from day one until after it was all over.

They had a flock of ships there, I'm telling you. That was really something. We bombarded there then for three or four days, just one right after the other, before we landed our people. Then we stayed there and we stayed there and we stayed there.*

Paul Stillwell: Were there kamikaze threats during this period?

Mr. Logue: Yes, sir, there were kamikazes, and we had one come right through there. We never did know whether that old boy got hit with our gunfire or whether he chickened out at too late a time, because apparently he had either fallen back or done something with his stick. But it came right across almost the quarterdeck of that ship, and his wings tore loose on the mainmast leg and the turret.† He went right through there and left his wings on our deck, and the fuselage and him went in the drink on the other side. Everybody was out there with tin snips cutting up those wings, and they were gone in no time at all. Souvenirs. Crazy nuts. That's the only kamikaze I know of and the closest we came.

---

*The ship's official history, prepared by the Navy Department, reports that the New York was under repairs at Manus for three weeks and then steamed alone to Okinawa. She arrived there on 27 March in preparation for the invasion on 1 April. She was in action for 76 consecutive days without relief.
†The tripod mainmast was just forward of turret number four. The Japanese suicide plane, which hit the ship on 14 April 1945, demolished a spotting plane on the turret four catapult.

Paul Stillwell: That's close, though.

Mr. Logue: Yes, it was. You know it was. That's an awful part of the ship to hit, too, right in there because you're right behind your firerooms and your engine rooms, right in the mess of that in there. Oh, shoot.

Paul Stillwell: Yes, if he'd had a bomb and it exploded on board the ship, the damage would have been much worse.

Mr. Logue: There you are. Tore out the whole midships part there. You know it was a funny thing--I don't mean to criticize this, but--Spruance, Admiral Spruance operated that thing, and he ran it, I thought, great, and he handled that all the way up till about the last two weeks. They pulled him in and sent Halsey out to finish it.*

Paul Stillwell: Right.

Mr. Logue: I suppose there's a reason for that.

Paul Stillwell: Well, they normally rotated them.

Mr. Logue: I see. Well, he only had about two weeks, but anyhow, none of my business, so I never worried about it, but he came out.
  Did you ever ride an old battleship when it fired all them guns at the same time?

Paul Stillwell: No.

---

*Admiral Raymond A. Spruance, USN, served as Commander Fifth Fleet during the Central Pacific campaign in 1944-45. On 27 May 1945, he was relieved as operational commander by Admiral William F. Halsey, Jr., USN, Commander Third Fleet. The same group of ships was known alternately as Fifth Fleet or Third Fleet, depending on which admiral was in command at the time.

Mr. Logue: Hey. That's an experience.

Paul Stillwell: What was it like?

Mr. Logue: Eaaahhh oooohhhhh--way back over like that. Back and forth for quite a ways, boy, I'll tell you. Now, it's bad enough when they fire one or two of them, but five of them, that really sends you.

Paul Stillwell: All five turrets.

Mr. Logue: All five turrets. That's full broadside, and oh boy. Anyhow, that's the only time I ever experienced that, and I didn't need any more of it either.

Paul Stillwell: Where was that? Was that at Okinawa?

[Interruption for change of tape]

Paul Stillwell: Well, you were in the midst of the Okinawa operation. Anything more to finish that up?

Mr. Logue: Not really. After they got that done, fenced her down pretty close, and then when they came in and finished it off, why, we went back up to Pearl Harbor. I mean, I think they were lobbing those shells out over end. That thing had been--for 76 days we bombarded. And every Wednesday we went over to Kerama Retto to get ammunition and more shells and then came back and every--Sunday and all we bombarded.* Whatever we were called on.

Paul Stillwell: Was fatigue a factor at that point?

---

*Kerama Retto is a group of small islands off the southwest coast of Okinawa. It was used as an anchorage and logistics base during the Okinawa campaign.

Mr. Logue: Somewhat, I think. That come nearer to it than anytime I ever had it in the Navy, and I probably had it easy down there where I was at compared to what some of them guys were doing up there. So I think, yes, it was fatigue because they took some of them off and sent them back.

Paul Stillwell: Well, you probably spent a lot of time at general quarters, didn't you?

Mr. Logue: Yes. Every day. We bombarded from daylight till dark. Then we pulled out to what they called the night steaming area until the next morning you were there. You had your breakfast about 4:00 in the morning before daylight. And then you ate the rest of it out of your little kit.

Paul Stillwell: Did you have C rations?

Mr. Logue: Yes. So the only hot meal we had was breakfast and that usually oatmeal or something like that.

Paul Stillwell: Well, what about the rations? Were they edible?

Mr. Logue: Not bad. As I recall they weren't too bad. We had pork and beans and we had--

Paul Stillwell: Spam probably.

Mr. Logue: Well, it might have been. It was some kind of meat, all right. I even had some potato chips and one thing and another. I was impressed. I thought from what I had heard of the earlier ones, they must have made some great improvements.

Paul Stillwell: I'll bet.

Mr. Logue: Because my only experience was that we had that was at Okinawa. Oh, you got tired of it, but then I'd hate to say anything too harsh about it, because I think it was probably under the circumstances as good as you could expect.

Paul Stillwell: Well, now, you talked about fear. How would the Okinawa campaign compare with, say, the convoys and some of the other things you had done in the ship?

Mr. Logue: Well, that particular experience I had mentioned kind of wore off. I don't think there was ever a day you didn't have some kind of fear till you got used to it. But it was still there. You're jumpy to a degree, and yet you couldn't afford to be jumpy, because a lot depended on what your job was and what was expected of you, and so I think that probably it tightened up your nerves. I don't know how to put it any better. But you just became accustomed, really, to what you were up against.

Sure, you knew the possibility every day and, but then you knew it every day and every day you lived, that was another day that it didn't happen. That's a long time back, but as near as I can remember I think we just kind of accepted it. I do kind of remember quite a letdown when you got out of something like that and got back into someplace like Pearl.

Paul Stillwell: Relaxation?

Mr. Logue: Yes. High point. I mean you--

Paul Stillwell: Not letdown in the sense of disappointment?

Mr. Logue: No, no, no. What do I want to say? I want to say that "Whew!! Hot dog."

Paul Stillwell: A sense of relief.

Mr. Logue: Relief. Yes, I want that better. We went back to Pearl to re-gun because we were getting ready for the invasion of Japan.* They took our big old guns out of them turrets and took them in for relining, and they got about two-thirds of the way through when the Japs surrendered.†

Paul Stillwell: Were you in dry dock at the time or at the pier?

Mr. Logue: I don't think we were in dry dock because we weren't working on the under part of the ship.

Paul Stillwell: Okay, so you were just at a pier at the navy yard?

Mr. Logue: Yes, and they were using cranes to take the tops off of the turrets and taking the big guns out and take them over to get them re-gunned and back. And then about halfway through with that when they surrendered, so they did put those guns back in. I don't think they ever finished relining them. I'm trying to think how this all come about now. They put us back together, and then they took out all of our ammunition, all of the powder, everything out of all those magazines and compartments. and they filled them with men and the first time we went back to Long Beach and we unloaded them.

Paul Stillwell: Had they put bunks in the magazines?

Mr. Logue: No, the bunks, cots, whatever they could get in there. Sleep on the floor, wherever. You want to go back to the States? You're going back.

Paul Stillwell: That's right.

---

*Operation Olympic was the code name for the Allied invasion of the Japanese island of Kyushu, scheduled for 1 November 1945.
†Hostilities in the war in the Pacific ended on 15 August 1945. The formal Japanese surrender was on 2 September on board the battleship Missouri (BB-63) in Tokyo Bay.

Mr. Logue: Well, what could you do?

Paul Stillwell: That's right.

Mr. Logue: There was no way you had time to set up a bunch of bunks and stuff like that. You know they took several ship loads of those guys out there. Now they all wanted to come back at once. So they were doing the best they could. I really had admiration for whoever lined that up. We made room for them on the decks wherever we could and got everybody on there we could because no more war. So we took them over there and unloaded that bunch at Long Beach.

Paul Stillwell: What do you remember about the news of the atomic bombs and then the end of the hostilities?[*]

Mr. Logue: Oh, man. I think we cried a little again, and I was invited up to the warrant officers' room along with the chiefs and everybody else. He broke out the bottle, so we all had a drink on that and talked about what we were going to do when we got home, I suppose. We talked about the war and how glad we were it was over and just that sort of thing that you'd expect.

Paul Stillwell: Probably even a bigger sense of relief than you'd felt getting away from the battle zone.

Mr. Logue: Oh, yes. Yes. Yes. Oh, shoot yes.

Paul Stillwell: You got a new skipper that year. What appealed to you about Captain Carter?

---

[*]In the first combat use of atomic bombs, U.S. B-29 bombers hit Hiroshima, on the island of Honshu, on 6 August 1945 and Nagasaki, on Kyushu, on 9 August.

Mr. Logue: Well, like I said, most captains when they come through, they're pretty strict, and that's what they have a captain's inspection for, to make sure that you're at your best. That's where you're supposed to look your best. Have your uniform just right--you're supposed to be able to stand just right. Everything that you should do, do it militarily. That's part of the training. That's part of being in the Navy. And this is what you are accustomed to.

Grayson B. Carter, when he come aboard he was a big Irishman, jovial, and happy with everyone. He was just liable to go by and slap you on the back if he saw you on the deck. "Hi, Son. How are you today?" or something like that.

When he came down through the captain's inspection, he had his helper right behind him with a camera, and he would come through and say, "This is a good-looking bunch. This is a fine-looking bunch, fine-looking sailors. Get that man's picture. I want that man's picture. I'm going to take that. You look fine, too, Son. Where are you from? Well, I'll declare. Well, that's fine." Just like that sort of an attitude. Why, you know, he just relaxed everybody as he went on through. It wasn't exactly what I'd call a captain's inspection, but it was what he called it, and so I just never had seen anybody do it that way. It was after the war, though, really, when he came aboard. We never had any more encounters, and I can't help but feel like that old boy was put on there for morale purposes, because it was getting pretty low along about then.

Paul Stillwell: Why?

Mr. Logue: Well, from everything that we had come through, and we were still out there and so forth, and I think that maybe somebody thought that was just the medicine that everybody needed. But, anyhow, that was unusual. All my career I never seen anybody come through a captain's inspection like that. He never had a bad thing to say to anybody. Just complimentary. "You guys have a nice day today now." And he'd go on to the next group that was lined up, you know. Same thing.

Paul Stillwell: But that's the kind of guy that you would really put out extra effort for.

Mr. Logue: I think so. I think so. But he was well liked.

Paul Stillwell: I can understand that.

Mr. Logue: Yes, sir. When he left the ship, where we were getting out toward the end of everything, I mean, practically the whole crew got up there and manned that rail around there to wave good-bye to the old boy.

Paul Stillwell: Respect.

Mr. Logue: You bet, and there was hardly anybody but what liked Grayson B. Carter. Yes, sir, he was a good Irishman.

Paul Stillwell: Had you made chief petty officer by the end of the war?

Mr. Logue: No. I never made chief. For one thing, I was going home, and I was going to have a family. I would have liked to have stayed and had my job, but I wanted that wife and that family worse. That's a decision I had to make, because I liked my job on the ship. There toward the last I really enjoyed the work I was doing. I felt comfortable in it, and I was learning new things all the time, and I really did like it. I liked the Navy much better. I got accustomed to it. I got along very well. But, again, I wanted to get home with that little wife, and I wanted some children. That was one thing we held off--till after the war--before we had any children. So that won out.

Paul Stillwell: I was just wondering how much turnover there was in the New York then? How many were there like you who were there from the beginning of the war to the end?

Mr. Logue: I've got a story to tell you on that. Might as well do it right now. When we got loaded up again, we went back through the canal and took a bunch over to New York.

Paul Stillwell: Do you have any memories of going through the Panama Canal?

Mr. Logue: Yes, yes. I can remember going through three times and you just go in till they float you up. Nothing that was to be outstanding or anything that you didn't already know about. I'd go topside so I could see it, and once you saw it you saw it. We generally hit a liberty on the other side and, boy, you saw some rotten things over there, I'll tell you.

Paul Stillwell: Such as?

Mr. Logue: Well, if you were looking for immorality, why, there was a street that was full of it. And maybe you thought you'd like to see something like that, but when you did you wish you hadn't.

Paul Stillwell: Sort of disgusting?

Mr. Logue: Oh, very. Very much so, yes. They just take them around the corner inside of a plate glass window, and you could go by and see what was going on. And just any way you wanted it, you got it. And so that was too much for me.

Paul Stillwell: Please tell me about being in New York City.

Mr. Logue: Oh, yes. We went in there, and we were in for Navy Day.[*] That's when they were waiting to see what they were going to do, and we were all lined up out there. That was just mainly it. And there was another cruiser, I think, or two. There were several ships in there.

Paul Stillwell: Well, there was close to 50, I think, altogether, just strung up the river.

---

[*] Navy Day was celebrated 27 October 1945 at various sites throughout the nation. Included was a long line of warships moored in the Hudson River off the west side of New York City.

Mr. Logue: I think you're right. I never did know how many for sure. But, of course, he went aboard the <u>Missouri</u>, and they said they give him a fried chicken dinner.* [Laughter] But I never criticized Harry. I kind of admired the guy for taking over where he did. It wasn't necessarily his party or anything like that. It had nothing to do with the party, as far as I was concerned. But, under the circumstances and at the time that he had to take the reins, in my own personal opinion, from what little I knew, I couldn't help but admire the guy.† So I was proud to stand up there for him, as I would have for anybody.

Paul Stillwell: Well, Navy Day was a cold windy day.

Mr. Logue: That's right.

Paul Stillwell: And your crew had to man the rail.

Mr. Logue: All of us did, and the thing of it was that every 30 minutes, I think, you could drop back against the side of the ship out of the wind. Smoke a cigarette if you wanted to. Keep it down low. And they would take ever so many ever so often this group and so on. They did that during dinner and stuff like that. As quick as he came out, back on the rail again. That was in the morning, and we didn't get off of that rail until I think about 1600, where they could get him clear out of there. And I don't think Harry would have ever liked that if he'd a known what was it was all about. Just the kind of guy that he appeared to me to be. I don't think he'd have liked it.

Paul Stillwell: Right.

Mr. Logue: But, I didn't feel bad about it. I really mean that because, like I said, I admired the guy; he was my commander in chief. You know, you get crazy, don't you? When you

---

*Harry S. Truman, a man from Missouri, was then President of the United States and decreed that the <u>Missouri</u> be the site of the Japanese surrender. His daughter Margaret had christened the ship in January 1944.
†Truman became President when Franklin D. Roosevelt died in office on 12 April 1945.

E. E. Logue (12/13/95) – Page 108

get in that outfit. It gets to you once in a while. No. I was a little bitter about it in some ways and yet kind of proud about it, too, to get to do that.

Paul Stillwell: I think the Missouri was moored right aft of the New York, wasn't she?

Mr. Logue: Yes.

Paul Stillwell: What do you remember about that ship?

Mr. Logue: I knew very little about it. Very little about it at all. Again, most of my time was below decks. It was a beautiful ship to look at. I would be very proud to serve on it had I been given an opportunity under the circumstances, but I really didn't know much about it or any of the new ones. I'd have been totally lost, I'm sure of that. [Laughter]

Paul Stillwell: Were the civilians hospitable to the Navy men there in New York City at that time?

Mr. Logue: Very much. Yes they were.

Paul Stillwell: Any examples you remember?

Mr. Logue: You bet. Oh, what was it now? They were friendly to you, and I know I went in with old John Diamond one time. We went in to a bar and ordered up; I always got a whiskey sour. That was not a very big drink and very much and I cold ease along on that to get by, and old John would get what he wanted.

One time we went into this bar; we got in there kind of early, and he wouldn't even charge us for the drinks. He let us have all we wanted and so forth, and you found quite a bit of that. And when we were going to school there, Mickey and I had an apartment down there not far and there was a grocery store. Now, she didn't have any ration stamps or anything with her--she just came loitering out there--and this guy knew that none of our wives had them. He'd sneak us a can of coffee every once in a while. Things like that he could do. And that's the best way I can express it. That's just the way they treated us. They were real nice to us.

I liked New York. I really did, because they were good to us and had a lot of wonderful places to see and do and all, and I think we saw every big band--Tommy Dorsey--everybody but Glenn Miller. He'd already gone over before we got in there. But Tommy and Jimmy Dorsey and all the whole bunch of them. It was a lot of fun.

Paul Stillwell: Did you have visitors on board your ship when you were there in New York?

Mr. Logue: Yes. Mickey came aboard after the war now when we come back that last time. She came with old Sarge and his wife. They came aboard, and she got to come down to the shop and see where I was at and so on and so forth. Yes, they got to do that. I'm glad you brought that up.

While we were there, the city and state New York was arguing about who was going to get it--like Texas got the Texas.* Finally, the Navy got tired of messing with them, and they wanted to take it to Bikini anyhow, so we went back through again, and we went to Pearl Harbor.† We got one day out of Pearl Harbor, and they turned that ship around and come back to San Francisco.

When I got back to San Francisco, I found out that my Dad had had a very serious stroke. Mr. Kelly was then our warrant officer. When I first knew him, he was second class Kelly. Mr. Kelly was a dandy fellow, a good man. He came down and he said, "Logue, bad news." He told me Dad had had this stroke, and he had my leave papers at the same time. He said, "You get home. You come back and be back here. We're going to sail." And he give me the date. "Be back here the night before." So I went home, spent that time with my Dad--last time I ever saw him too. God, I was glad I got to go.

Came back, went back into the ship, and went down into the light shop, which was my area. There were three guys I never saw before in my life and one more outside there.

---

*The battleship Texas (BB-35) has been a memorial on display in the San Jacinto State Park, near Houston, Texas, since April 1948.
†In July 1946 a joint Army-Navy task force conducted tests at Bikini Atoll in the Marshall Islands to determine the effects of atomic bombs on moored warships. Along with an array of U.S. ships were captured German and Japanese warships.

I looked around for somebody I might know, and there wasn't anybody. Pretty soon somebody spoke up and said, "Are you Logue?"

I said, "Yeah, where is everybody?"

He said, "We're everybody."

"Well, what are you talking about?"

Well, it so happened that Congress had suddenly passed a law that everybody that was eligible to get out, right now you let them out. And they did. They had to bring that ship back to Frisco. They let off all the guys that were working for me. They went home. Can't blame them for that, but what a spot. Those guys didn't know where the first light switch was, and we're getting under way. So we had a time, I want to tell you.

We went out then to Pearl and put off everything except the very clothes and stuff we would need at Bikini. I want to tell you, that's the most efficient I ever saw the Navy in my life, and I'll tell you why when I come back. Well, we took them over there, and they had great big buildings there full of our stuff in there in seabags and whatever bags we had there to go with us.

So we went on then out to Bikini, and they anchored us at our spot, to where we would be in line with all of the others. When they got ready to drop the first one, why, of course, we all had to abandon ship.* We went over to the passenger ship that they had brought out there for us. We were 20 miles out and we could see the first bomb. It was the one that was in the air. Well, the wind soon carried it away, and it was safe they took us and put us back on the ship the same day. That evening we got back on again.

Paul Stillwell: Was there a concern about radiation hazard?

Mr. Logue: No, they checked it out. I don't think there was, and, of course, you didn't have any choice but to have faith. I mean, if those guys said it was all right, far as I'm concerned it had to be all right. I mean, there's no use worrying about it. I mean, you can worry yourself sick. What's the use? I mean, you're there. You're working. You're going to have to do it. So I don't think they ever steered us wrong. If they did, I never knew it.

---

*The first test, the air burst, was on 1 July 1946.

But the second time, which was several weeks later, was down below the water.* It looked like water was going up and coming down at the same time there for quite a little while before that got straightened out. And it just soaked the outside of that ship with the radioactivity, so it was probably three or four weeks before anybody could get aboard.

Paul Stillwell: And you were staying on this troop transport?

Mr. Logue: All this time. That's true. What they had--they said anyhow--was that they used these fire boats, you know, that they used to put out fires. They had boiler compound and lye water was the combination that I understand they used and they sprayed that old ship--went around and round and round it. About every third day they'd come and do that, and they did that for about three or four weeks. Finally, the old man couldn't stand it any longer. We had a commander this time, and he'd been the first lieutenant, and they took the captain and the commander, the executive officer, clear off the ship and left it with this guy to go out to Bikini. He wasn't a bad old guy. Don't misunderstand me. I mean, that this was what we were cut down to.

Paul Stillwell: You must not have had a very big crew in this ship at that time.

Mr. Logue: No. Skeleton crew and I had to teach those kids every day. Oh, I was going to tell you. One night about midnight I got a telephone call. I'd been working day and night anyhow, trying to get lined out, and I heard this voice on there. He said, "I can't get my electric razor to work in the socket here, and an officer wants to shave."

I said, "Sir, there's an enlisted man down there that wants to sleep." And I hung up. That's the only time in my life I ever did a thing like that. I was so dad-gummed plumb tired I didn't care if they hung me off the yardarm. And I was just waiting the next morning. I knew I'd get a repercussion from it, and I just waited to see what it was. So I went to quarters, and after quarters, why, Kelly cornered me and he said, "I understand that was an officer that wanted to shave last night."

I said, "Yes, sir."

---
*The underwater explosion was on 25 July 1946.

"Well, Logue," he said, "I can't admire the way you handled it, but I can't blame you. I talked to the chief engineer, and he talked to the ensign." So he said, "It won't happen again." Well, they knew what we were up against and--blast it all--a lot of that stuff they eased up on, because they knew you were doing your best. So they were human and we made it, just because we had people like that aboard that were willing to work with you and help you.

Paul Stillwell: Well, what happened after the second blast and then the high water and all that?

Mr. Logue: Finally, they sent me and two other guys aboard, that we might go down and into the forward part of the ship. We had taken those batteries off in the meantime and brought some small diesel engine driven dynamos for the emergency power. They wanted me to run casualty power from there clear on up to the boiler rooms, so they could get the boiler started and get up a head of steam. What this old man thought he was doing, I don't know. Whether he thought he was going to take it back to the States or what.

But, anyhow, these were the orders, so I took my crew and went over and then several other divisions sent a few guys over for various things. When you got topside, you looked, and there'd be a big old chalked circle like this that said, "Two Hours." Maybe this one over here would say, "Three Hours." Maybe back over here, "Thirty Minutes." And, of course, that was the tolerance you had. You could be that long out of every 24 hours without getting damaged. Well, we got below. There was nothing down there--except maybe down in the shafts or something like that you had to watch for. So we went down and started to work, and we spent the night there after we worked as long as we could and then got up the next morning and started again.

Then here come Mr. Kelly with his group. He said, "You guys get back over and get some sleep." Which we did. Then this went on, because we had to come back then that afternoon, and again I was getting myself in all kinds of trouble or I should have, because I'd always been very careful to be courteous. I mean, that's part of your training. That's part of your job. And I always was. But we're back there at past midships, toward the after part, and went down into an area down there in front of the chiefs' quarters. We had to get down there and find out where to hook that cable in down below. I sent one man down there with a light, and I was instructing him from up above and this other guy at the same time. And in the meantime, why, here come someone. Now, they had these slick-arm chiefs.* Do you remember them?

Paul Stillwell: I've heard of them.

Mr. Logue: Well, they weren't the most popular in the world. I mean, some of us guys worked pretty hard to even get where we were at, and they come along and slap chief on--well, that's here nor there. I guess it was important, or they wouldn't have done it. They wanted them for what they knew. And that's all I could see was just that bare arm. This guy come up there and said, "Sparky, how you getting along. Are you ever going to get that finished?"

I said, "I'm a blankety-blank-blank electrician, not a magician."

He said, "Well, there's just this thing about it. If you need something else, you get ahold of your captain and have him get ahold of me. I'll see that you get what you need. We need to get this done." About that time, as he turned around, I saw that he was an admiral. "Yes, sir, Admiral." [Laughter] And he just went on. He never cussed me out or anything. That was it. But I want to tell you, I looked them over after that.

Paul Stillwell: You thought he was a chief?

Mr. Logue: Yes. Ho, ho, ho. No, that had nothing to do with my being chief. The reason I didn't go up for chief was because by the time I had enough time in in first class to go up for chief, I knew I was getting out, and I couldn't make enough money extra on what wages I'd get between the two to even buy my uniforms. So I couldn't figure any point in going--all the trouble of going up for chief. I was going home when the time come, so it wasn't long then till I left.

---

*A "slick-arm" chief petty officer would be one who had no hashmarks on his sleeve, meaning he had been in the Navy for less than four years. In the period before the war it took many years to make chief, but with the rapid wartime expansion of the Navy, some men did it on their first enlistment.

Paul Stillwell: Well, you probably felt a sense of affection for the ship by then.

Mr. Logue: Certainly I did, and I'm not real proud she's laying way down there at the bottom.* I think David probably gave me the best turn of things on that.† For years I could just see her down there with the dadgum crab grabbing on her you know and rusting and all that sort of thing.

He said, "Well, was it in deep water where they sunk her?"

I said, "I just imagine it was. I don't know." But he said if it was down there deep enough, it looks just like it did when it went down.

Paul Stillwell: Right.

Mr. Logue: And that gave me a good feeling anyhow.

Paul Stillwell: Well, for the ones that were cut up there's nothing left.

Mr. Logue: And so I don't know. What difference does it make? Yet like you said, it was home, and it saved my life a lot of times, and I did my best for her, so I don't know. Does that sound crazy?

Paul Stillwell: No. A lot of people feel that way about their ships. Probably by the time you left were not many of the people who had been aboard when you joined.

Mr. Logue: That's true. That's true.

Paul Stillwell: Well, were you there when was she was actually sunk?

---

*On 8 July 1948, following a pounding by ships and aircraft of the Pacific Fleet, the New York capsized and sank some 40 miles out from Pearl Harbor, Hawaii.
†This is a reference to Captain David Durbin, JAGC, USNR, a friend of Mr. Logue. The interview took place in Durbin's office.

Mr. Logue: No. I was going to tell you. My time was coming up, and so Kelly said, "Logue, you're going home."

Paul Stillwell: When was that?

Mr. Logue: That was out at Bikini.

Paul Stillwell: Well, what month maybe, August?

Mr. Logue: Let me think now. Yes, it would have been August of '46, because my time would have been up December the second of 1946. But, oh, I mean, they were looking for people. People were getting out. They'd had enough, you know, and they wanted out and got out, those that could. So they took me back to Frisco, then sent me back down to San Pedro. Then they put me out on the Pasadena, and I served then on the Pasadena for I think two or three weeks is about all. It was going out, and they couldn't talk me into shipping over, so they put me over on the Columbus.* And I made a hit there.

They had all the cease-fire connections in all these boxes. All the cease-fire boxes were open wired--just like they come out of the Navy yard that way--clear down to the central station to where the main line--all wires everywhere. So this division officer was Mr. Byers, who was a full lieutenant. I'll never forget; he said, "Man, you're just the man I'm looking for. I want you to get you some help. I want all them hooked up."

I said, "Well, we'll do our best." So I got ahold of a fellow by the name Armentrout, I think his last name was--Army we called him--and we got a couple of sound-powered phones.

So I went down into central station, and I took him out where I wanted him to start, which was the first box away. These sound-powered phones had the clamps on them, and I said, "You get on there, and I want you to put your ground wire on the ground, and one at a time I want you to get on those wires and talk to me." And as quick as I heard him, I hollered, "Hold it right there. Put that on number one." And I'd put mine on number one. We did that to every box, and it took us three solid weeks, every day, but we got her done.

---

*Pasadena (CL-65) and Columbus (CA-74) were new cruisers.

They tested it and you know what they did? The ship was getting ready to go up to, oh, just north of--oh, what's that town up north there? I can't think but anyhow it was north of Los Angeles quite a little ways. Not Frisco or anything like that but up north there a ways, anchored out, and they were going to go up there. This was Thursday, and Lieutenant Byers come along and said, "You and Army have got leave from now until Monday up there." And turned us loose, so we went over and had all that time. I knew it was just because he was pleased with the job. So then when it came time for me to get off, why, they couldn't hold me any longer. And he wanted me to ship over so darn bad.[*] He would have been a nice guy to work with and on a nice ship. I liked it and all, but I just couldn't do it. Mickey had been waiting for this for years, and so had I.

Paul Stillwell: Yes, you'd been in for six years.

Mr. Logue: That's right, and so I told him I couldn't do it, so he'd razz me then and say, "Well, you know when you get out, the Republicans are back in again." He must have been a Democrat. He said, "Republicans back in again you know what'll happen then. You're going to have another depression."

I said, "Yeah, but when you guys get out to Asia," which is where they were headed for the Asiatic fleet, "When you guys get out there, there isn't going to be enough money to bring you back. I'm going home." [Laughter]

Well, we had a lot of fun over it, but then he said, "If you'll go home today, right now, this minute, whatever, you go home and be back here the day before we sail, I'll be standing on this bridge with a chief's cap for you."

I said, "I don't want mine that way. If I was going to get it, that isn't the way I want it. I took my course like everybody else, but I'm getting out." So we shook hands and all, and that was it. I went on, but, bless his heart, I felt sorry for him. There wasn't anybody left.

Paul Stillwell: Right.

---

[*] "Ship over" is a Navy slang term meaning to reenlist for any additional term of duty.

Mr. Logue: The old-timers probably had figured on staying for 20 or 30 years, but they got out. They had enough, and that was just the way it was. So I went over then to the station at San Pedro. Oh, they were snotty to you over there because you wouldn't ship over. They just treated you like dirt. They said that they would pay us for all but 60 days, and they would let us go 60 days early--this was what Congress put out--and then pay us for the rest. Gosh, I had 200 days of leave or something like that coming. So you know what he did? He just kept me sitting in there. He extended my enlistment two months, and I sat in there an extra two months. In other words, they let me go at my regular time, which would have been the second of December, and they should have let me go two months before. They let me go then and extended my enlistment to the second of February and mailed me my discharge.

Paul Stillwell: How did you spend that time?

Mr. Logue: Well, Mickey was there and I could get over every night, and so it wasn't all that bad in a way. But yet is sure galled me to think that a guy who does his best for them for six years, and that's the thank you, but then I knew that wasn't reflecting the Navy. It was reflecting these particular guys that was mad because we was going home and they weren't.

Paul Stillwell: That's exactly it.

Mr. Logue: That's it. So that was it and that's my naval career.

Paul Stillwell: Well, in a few sentences why don't you summarize what happened after that? How did you spend the rest of your life?

Mr. Logue: Well, we went home. Are you ready for this? Looking back on it, it's kind of different. I went home and the first job I had was picking up corn behind a corn picker, which they didn't have corn pickers when I was on the farm. And that didn't last very long. Next I got a job working at a hay outfit that they went out and cut the hay and took it in.

They had a big old tumbler and they cooked the hay until it got just dry enough to where they could grind it into meal and bagged it and put in a boxcar. So I got a job driving a truck and I did that for several weeks so finally he says, "You're going to be the new boss down here on this shift. You're going to run that."

"I don't know the first thing about it."

"You're going to learn right now." So he taught me how to operate that big thing, you know, and I had two guys on the dock working for me and loading the car, so I come about fall then I said, "What are we going to do this winter?"

He said, "I don't even know what I'm going to do this winter." And the next thing you know, the grocery store--I'm living in this little town of Bentley now--we've bought a little old house there when I first got out of the Navy--and the guy in the grocery store said, "How would like to come work in the grocery store?" Just out of the clear blue sky.

Well, it was a job and that was better than I was going to have, so I said, "What do you pay?"

He said, "A hundred and fifty dollars a month and 10% percent off on your groceries. That's six days a week and on till 9:00 o'clock every other Saturday. That wasn't too bad for a country town at that time, so at least it was a living. And so I took it. So I worked for him then for about a year, year and a half, and here come the school board, and they wanted to hire me to be a janitor at the high school. That was the one I graduated out of. And they offered me $200.00 a month, and it would be 40-hour week except working--it was my responsibility to do the janitorial work during the day, and maybe I'd get in that number, maybe not that much, maybe over, whatever, but whatever work it was during the summer it was 40 hours. So I took that.

Well, that made the grocery man mad. I couldn't help that, so I worked at that then for probably a year and a half or two years and I thought, "Hey. Where's this getting me? A little rinky-dink town out here. And there aren't any jobs out here." So the government said that they'd give us a chance at some education, so I went down at Wichita Business College. That's the only thing Wichita had. I really wanted to be a barber. Now, that sounds crazy but I'd have had to go to Tulsa, Oklahoma City, or Denver, or Kansas City. I couldn't do that. I couldn't afford to move my family or nothing, so I went down and I took first part accounting. Well, they come in there and whenever there were jobs, why, they would announce it for us guys, so they said there's a service station down here at 29th and Arkansas that is looking for a part-time man. Anybody that interested.

I said, "I am. I'll go out there this evening." So I did. I got on. So I worked for him until I finished first part accounting, and I saw I wasn't going to be an accountant and there wasn't any use of wasting the government's money, and he offered me a full-time job there which was better money that I'd made yet, so I worked there six days a week. And there was a refinery over just about a mile east of us, and we selling their gas anyhow, and all the guys were trading there. I got acquainted with the superintendent of the refinery, and I asked him, "Do you ever hire guys over there at the refinery?" That would have been a nice job and it was.

He said, "Well, yeah. When we need one."

I said, "Would you want to keep me in mind?"

"Yeah," he said. "I've watched you work around here and I think you'd make us a good man. Yeah, I sure will."

It wasn't but two or three weeks he come along on a Friday and he said, "I need you Monday."

I said, "Oh. I ought to tell old--I'd like to give old Paul Kline, the boss there, a little bit of time."

He said, "Well, I don't blame you. I'd like to see you do that, but I have to have a man Monday."

I said, "Hang on just a minute, will you?" So I went in and told Paul. Paul said, "You take that job." He said, "We'll get a service station man in here, but you don't get a job like that every day. You take that job."

Well, I thanked him and I went out and told him. I went to work for him Monday. I worked for him two years. They shut that place down. But I happened to have a friend in the office, and when Phillips Petroleum called out there and heard that they was letting guys go they wanted to hire a man. He said, "I got just the man." They sent me down. They hired me. I worked for Phillips for 23 years, and then Phillips shut down. And one of the jobbers for some reason liked me real well happened to be the chairman of the Authority Board of the Kansas Turnpike Authority. He came in there and he said, "What are you going to do?"

I said, "I wish I knew."

He said, "How would you like to work for the turnpike?"

I said, "Best offer I've had yet."

"Well," he said. "I don't know what you're going to do but you got a job." I worked for the turnpike then for 13 years till I retired, so that's my history after I got out.

Paul Stillwell: That's great. Well, please tell me about this family that you raised after you got out.

Mr. Logue: Okay. When we first got out, why, Larry come along October just pretty darn soon after we got out--that was maybe just a little short of a year.

Paul Stillwell: So October '47.

Mr. Logue: October of '47. His birthday is October 12th, because Mike's is October the 11th, about five, six years later. But Larry come along, and, oh, he was a wonderful kid. He was easy to raise and good looking like me and-- [Laughter]

Paul Stillwell: Well, that says it all.

Mr. Logue: And Larry now, of course, is, as you know, pastor of the Pittman church over there now. He's a good Christian boy and good pastor and we can't be more proud of him. Michael came along. He was the quietest kid you ever knew. Once in a while he'd ask a question, but when he did it was the derndest thing--I mean you'd wonder where in the world--how'd that come out of his head, you know? But I just wondered, you know, what in the world's ever going to happen to that guy. Well, he's in charge of the ice company there in Wichita, head man down there now on salary, and he's the president of the school board at Valley Center, and he's just doing real great.

Paul Stillwell: Great.

Mr. Logue: He's a splendid young man, if I do say so myself. I couldn't have two finer boys. Those boys are very, very attentive to us. Larry will give us a call at least once every two weeks. Mike checks in on us at least twice a week. Not necessary. We're both healthy. Getting along fine, but they just want to do that so I don't know how you're going to beat it.

Paul Stillwell: Well, the decision that you made to get out and have a family really paid off.

Mr. Logue: I think so, and my wife and I were madly in love--still are--and we've had a wonderful life. We've still got it.

Paul Stillwell: That's great.

Mr. Logue: I couldn't ever be happier and that's just about it, for the truth. This will be the first night that I've missed being with my wife since back in 1950s when I went back into the reserves. I went back into the reserves and they put me on recruiting duty. And then when I come out of that, I quit.

Paul Stillwell: What years were you in the reserve?

Mr. Logue: I'm trying to think now. Times were hard, and I was needing more money. I went down and talked to them, and they were glad to get me. But they didn't have any billet for me really except I was going to be the master-at-arms. If they had anybody call up anybody, why, it would be my responsibility to get them together and get them lined out and see that they got squared away take them down to the depot and kiss them goodbye and that stuff--whatever would be the duty on that--plus at the same time they gave me the Navy vehicle. Shoot, it was a whale of a deal. Thursday night was the meeting night. He said, "I don't care whether you work Thursday or Tuesday or whatever night it is. Just whatever night you think's best to go out. Just make sure you're in uniform and get the car and get out there and start hustling." I brought in quite a few, and I know I made a lot of enemies but then--

Paul Stillwell: Was this during the Korean War?

Mr. Logue: Yes. Yes, it was. But it got cooled down before I got out. And when it come time for me to get out, what was the deal on that? I think we were about to get into Vietnam War, if I'm not mistaken. Anyhow, I got out when I did at a safe time, which probably saved my neck. But, I'm getting old enough then that I think I could have got by. Oh, I've had a wonderful life. Still got a wonderful life.

Paul Stillwell: Well, I'm grateful to you for sharing it this afternoon and grateful to Mr. Durbin for suggesting it and making his office available..

Mr. Logue: I guess I am, too, because I've enjoyed it. I've worked my jaws. Incidentally, I came to the Lord many years ago, now 1950, give up my smoking and everything. I even became a pastor and I pastored two different churches for a while and then finally at 65 I quit all it. I still go out. I even had to hold a revival here a while back--a weekend revival for a little church out there at Melvern.

Paul Stillwell: You're certainly versatile.

Mr. Logue: I don't know about that, but it was--

Paul Stillwell: Well, please accept my apologies and thanks for this separation from your wife.

Mr. Logue: No problem. No problem. I kind of looked forward to it and I was scared of it, too, in a way. Everybody's got the bad times and the good times. I think probably one of the toughest times was losing Dad. I wanted him to be there when I came home and lost

Mother when I was 14. I had him a long time, and he was a great dad. He was a dandy and I got his fiddle. He insisted that I be the one to get his fiddle and I had my own guitar.

He and I played around at a lot of different places. Well, the old schoolhouses then, country schoolhouses. One Saturday night a month they would have some kind of a wing-ding and take lunch in everything like that. Shoot, we just made the circuits. I think they'd call us and want us to come out, and we'd put on a little show and he'd play. He could take some cattle ribs that he went out in the pasture and found an old skeleton and got them--he rattled those things like a drummer. I could never do that, but he did. He was good and I'd pick out a march or a melody or something on a guitar--play it, you know--and he'd rattle at that and oh, they liked that, you know.

So we had a lot of time together after Mom died and farmed together and all till we moved into town. But I can be so thankful for the family I had--for the mother and dad I had--brothers and sisters that I had and kind of tough to see them go one by one. My brother Paul, why, I lost him this April. I have one sister left. I think I probably told you that. She's got Alzheimer's and doesn't know anything or anybody now. But I'm thankful we went back. In May or June we took a plane back to see her there at Sacramento.

That's when it took me six hours to get from Kansas City to Sacramento. They come down and picked me up, and she knew me. I think that thrilled me more than it did her, but she knew me and we had a real good time together. Then we spent a week there with my niece, her daughter, and it thrilled her, too, that Daisy knew me and we had a real--I'll tell you. She kissed me every five minutes in there for a while, and I was her baby brother. And then after we left, why, then she told us here just recently that she didn't even know her daughter now or anything. But she's not unhappy. I mean, she doesn't know any more than that.

Paul Stillwell: Well, what I've heard demonstrates what I've heard from a lot of people. That you mostly remember the good times.

Mr. Logue: That's right.

Paul Stillwell: That's the way it should be.

Mr. Logue: Yes, sir, you're exactly right there. The bad times--and there were some--I know there was. I just don't remember them in a way that I could describe them. So you're just exactly right and I'm glad it's that way--like you said--I really am. Because I've got good memories; you can tell that on there.

Paul Stillwell: Sure.

Mr. Logue: Even in the Navy. A six-year stint--I really am proud of the time that I was able to be in. Like to feel like maybe somehow, someway I even contributed a little bit, but nevertheless I did what they told me to do, and that's all you know what to do.

Paul Stillwell: Well, you've made another contribution this afternoon and I thank you for that as well.

Mr. Logue: Well, Paul, thank you.

Index to the Oral History of
Mr. Elda Elwood Logue

Accidents
   The battleship New York (BB-34) ran aground in late 1941 and had to be dry-docked at Norfolk for repairs, 55-57

Alcohol
   Drinking in World War II by crew members of the battleship New York (BB-34), 52-53, 103

Atomic Bombs
   The battleship New York (BB-34) was one of the targets for the testing of atomic bombs in July 1946 at Bikini Atoll in the Marshall Islands, 110-114

Baumberger, Lieutenant (junior grade) Walter H., USN (USNA, 1934)
   Showed kindness to Logue in 1941 while serving as M division officer in the battleship New York (BB-34), 43-45

Bikini Atoll, Marshall Islands
   The battleship New York (BB-34) was one of the targets for the testing of atomic bombs in July 1946 at Bikini, 110-114

Carter, Captain Grayson B., USN (USNA, 1919)
   Popular skipper who commanded the battleship New York (BB-34) in 1945-46, 103-105

Christian, Captain Kemp C., USN (USNA, 1914)
   Activities while in command of the battleship New York (BB-34) from 1943 to 1945, 55, 78-81

Columbus, USS (CA-74)
   Shortly after World War II Logue worked in this sip to get the sound-powered telephone system squared away, 115-116

Convoys
   During World War II, the battleship New York (BB-34) escorted merchant ship convoys to Europe, 60, 62-65

Crossroads, Operation
   The battleship New York (BB-34) was one of the targets for the testing of atomic bombs in July 1946 at Bikini Atoll in the Marshall Islands, 110-114

Demobilization
    Rapid departure of many crew members of the battleship New York (BB-34) once World War II ended, 109-110

Farming
    By the Logue family in California and the Midwest in the 1920s and 1930s, 2-7, 9-11, 14; use of irrigation in Kansas, 10-11

Food
    Quality of at Great Lakes Naval Training Station in the early1940s, 24-25; messing arrangements in the early 1940s on board the battleship New York (BB-34), 83-84; the crew of the New York ate C rations in 1945, during the Okinawa campaign, 100-101

Ford, Henry
    Famous auto maker who in the early 1940s sponsored a school in Dearborn, Michigan, to train Navy machinist's mates, 28-30

Ford Motor Company
    In the early 1940s the company conducted a school at Dearborn, Michigan, to train Navy machinist's mates, 28-30

Gambling
    On board the battleship New York (BB-34) during World War II, 84-86

Great Lakes, Illinois, Naval Training Station
    Site of recruit training for Logue in the early 1940s, 18-26; site of a recruit's suicide in the early 1940s, 20; quality of food, 24-25; inspections, 25-26; machinist's mate training in 1941, 27-28

Gunnery—Naval
    Complement of guns on board the battleship New York (BB-34) at the beginning of World War II, 47-48, 54; in 1943-44 the New York served as a gunnery training ship on the East Coast, 77; the New York provided gunfire support during the invasions of Iwo Jima and Okinawa in early 1945, 93-101; partial re-gunning of the New York's main battery at Pearl Harbor in the summer of 1945, 102

Hammocks
    Difficulties learning to sleep in one in the early 1940s during recruit training at Great Lakes, Illinois, 19-20, 23

Hart, Admiral Thomas Charles, USN (USNA, 1897)
    While he was in command of the Asiatic Fleet in 1941, his son was an ensign in the battleship New York (BB-34), 43

Hart, Ensign Thomas Comins, USN (USNA, 1939)
   Showed kindness to Logue in 1941 while serving as E division officer in the battleship New York (BB-34), 43-45

Inspections
   During recruit training in the early 1940s at Great Lakes, Illinois, 25-26; Captain Grayson B. Carter made a point of being complimentary during inspections on board the battleship New York (BB-34) when he was in command in 1945-46, 104-105

Iwo Jima, Bonin Islands
   Invaded in February 1945 with support from the battleship New York (BB-34), 93-95

Japanese Navy
   During the Okinawa campaign, the battleship New York (BB-34) was hit and damaged on 14 April 1945 by a Japanese kamikaze aircraft, 97-98

Jean Bart (French Battleship)
   Role in defending against the Allied invasion of French Morocco in November 1942, 72-73

Kamikazes
   During the Okinawa campaign, the battleship New York (BB-34) was hit and damaged on 14 April 1945 by a Japanese kamikaze aircraft, 97-98

Kwajalein Atoll, Marshall Islands
   The battleship New York (BB-34) lost a propeller blade in late 1944 while en route to Kwajalein, 92-93

Leave and Liberty
   For students at machinist's mate school in Dearborn, Michigan, in 1941, 33-34; in New England towns in 1941 for crew members from the battleship New York (BB-34), 50-53; in late 1941 Logue's shipmates in the New York, which was dry-docked in Norfolk, took up a collection for him so he could go home on leave to Kansas, 57-59; in Scotland, early in World War II, 60-61, 66-67; role of the shore patrol, 67-68; at the end of 1942 in New York City, 71-72; in the Caribbean during World War II, 90-91; in Panama shortly after the end of World War II, 105-106

Logue, Elda Elwood
   Parents of, 1-7, 9-10, 12, 16-17, 19, 24, 27, 59, 70, 109, 122-123; other relatives, 1-3, 5, 10-14, 16, 45, 123; boyhood in California, Missouri, and Kansas in the 1920s and 1930s, 1-7, 9-14; education in Kansas in the 1930s, 7-9; wife Bertha Mae, 11-13, 15-17, 27, 59, 69-72, 76-77, 89-91, 105, 108-109, 116-117, 121; construction work in the late 1930s, 14-15; musical experiences, 16-17, 33, 123; enlistment in the Navy in late 1940, 17-18; recruit training in 1940-41 at Great Lakes, Illinois, 18-26; in 1941 took machinist's mate training at Great Lakes, Illinois, and Dearborn,

Michigan, 27-36; service from 1941 to 1946 on board the battleship New York (BB-34), 37-115; marriage in 1941 to Bertha Mae Maxwell, 69-72; studied gyrocompasses while in school in Brooklyn in late 1942, 69, 75-75; service in the cruisers Pasadena (CL-65) and Columbus (CA-74) shortly after World War II, 115-116; departure from the Navy in 1947 after six years of service, 116-117; civilian employment from 1947 until retirement in 1986, 117-120; children of, 120-121; service in the Naval Reserve following World War II, 121-122

Manus, Admiralty Islands
The battleship New York (BB-34) spent time in a floating dry dock in March 1945 to get damaged propellers replaced, 93-93, 97

Marine Corps, U.S.
Members of the Marine detachment in the battleship New York (BB-34) in World War II, 89-91

Marshall Islands
The battleship New York (BB-34) lost a propeller blade in late 1944 while en route to Kwajalein Atoll, 92-93; the New York was one of the targets for the testing of atomic bombs in July 1946 at Bikini, 110-114

Merchant Ships
During World War II, the battleship New York (BB-34) escorted merchant ship convoys to Europe, 60, 62-65

Mississippi, USS (BB-41)
The crew of this battleship was unfriendly to transient sailors on board in 1941 for short periods, 37-39

Music
In the late 1930s and early '40s, Logue sang on a radio station in Kansas, 16-17; Logue played in a small swing band when he took machinist's mate training in 1941, 33; Logue's experiences singing with his father, 123

Naval Reserve, U.S.
Logue's service as a reservist in the 1940s and 1950s, 121-122

Newport, Rhode Island
Site of liberty in late 1941 for crew members from the battleship New York (BB-34), 50-51

New York City
Liberty attractions for sailors in late 1942, 71-72; role of the Navy receiving station at Pier 91 on the city's west side during World War II, 76-77; in October 1945 a parade of ships moored in the Hudson River to observe Navy Day, 106-108; civilians were friendly and generous to sailors in World War II, 108-109

New York Navy Yard, Brooklyn, New York
Site of a Navy training school on gyrocompasses conducted during World War II, 69, 74-75

New York, USS (BB-34)
Battleship that conducted early radar tests in 1941, 38; in the 1940s had an oil-burning reciprocating, triple-expansion steam propulsion plant, 39-42; Logue's transfer in 1941 to the E division, 43-45; messing and berthing arrangements in the early 1940s, 45-46, 83-84, 91-92; work of the electrician's mates in the light shop in the early 1940s, 46-49, 78-81, 86-90, 93-96; gunnery capability at the beginning of World War II, 47-48, 54; operations and port visits on the East Coast in the latter part of 1941, 50-54; commanding officers during World War II, 54-57, 72-73, 78-81, 103-105; ran aground in late 1941 and had to be dry-docked at Norfolk for repairs, 55-57; convoy operations to Europe early in World War II, 59-65; the ship had a few black mess personnel in the crew, 61-62; short patrol duty for crew members, 67-68; role of senior enlisted men in training juniors, 69; role in supporting the invasion of French Morocco in November 1942, 72-73; role as an East Coast training ship in 1943-44 for gunnery and midshipman cruises, 77, 82-83; gambling on board the ship during World War II, 84-86; relationship between officers and enlisted men, 88-89; Marine detachment, 89-91; lost a propeller blade in late 1944 while en route to Kwajalein Atoll, 92-93, 97; provided gunfire support during the invasions of Iwo Jima and Okinawa in early1945, 93-101; the ship operated floatplanes, 95-96; damaged by a Japanese kamikaze plane off Okinawa in April 1945, 97-98; partial re-gunning of the ship's main battery at Pearl Harbor in the summer of 1945, 102; after World War II ended in 1945, the ship took servicemen from the Western Pacific to Long Beach, California, 102-103; in the autumn of 1945 passed through Panama en route to New York, 105-106; at Navy Day celebration at New York City in October 1945, 106-108; rapid departure of many crew members following the end of World War II, 109-110; ship was one of the targets for the testing of atomic bombs in July 1946 at Bikini Atoll in the Marshall Islands, 110-114; sinking of in 1948, 114

Norfolk, Virginia
The battleship New York (BB-34) ran aground in late 1941 and had to be dry-docked at Norfolk for repairs, 55-57; near-fight in a Norfolk bar during World War II, 68

Nuclear Weapons
See: Atomic Bombs

Okinawa, Ryukyus Islands
Invaded in April 1945 with support from the battleship New York (BB-34), 95-100; during the Okinawa campaign, the New York was hit and damaged on 14 April 1945 by a Japanese kamikaze aircraft, 97-101

Oliver, Electrician George A., USN
Served in the crew of the battleship New York (BB-34) during World War II, 79-81

Pearl Harbor, Hawaii
Partial re-gunning of the main battery of the battleship New York (BB-34) at Pearl Harbor in the summer of 1945, 102

Propulsion Plants
The battleship New York (BB-34) had a reciprocating, triple-expansion steam propulsion plant, 39-42; prior to the 1940s the New York's boilers were converted from coal to oil, 48-49; the New York lost a propeller blade in late 1944 while en route to Kwajalein Atoll, 92-93; repair at Manus in March 1945, 97

Recruit Training
Conducted in the early 1940s at Great Lakes, Illinois, 18-26

Scotland
Greenock and Glasgow provided hospitable places for visits by the crews of the battleship New York (BB-34) during World War II, even though they were hard hit by the war, 60-61, 66-67

Shore Patrol
Performed during World War II by crew members from the battleship New York (BB-34), 67-68

Training
Boot camp conducted in the early 1940s at Great Lakes, Illinois, 18-26; machinist's mate school in 1941 was conducted at Great Lakes, Illinois, and Dearborn, Michigan, 27-29; in the early 1940s the Ford Motor Company conducted a school at Dearborn, Michigan, to train Navy machinist's mates, 28-36; in the early 1940s the Navy conducted a school on gyrocompasses at the New York Navy Yard, 69, 74-75; in 1943-44 the battleship New York (BB-34) served as a training ship on the East Coast for gunnery and midshipman cruises, 77, 82-83

Truman, President Harry S.
Visited the fleet at New York City in October 1945 to observe Navy Day, 107-108

Umstead, Captain Scott, USN (USNA, 1915)
Commanded the battleship New York (BB-34) in 1942-43, including the period during the invasion of French Morocco, 55, 72-73

Ware, Captain James G., USN (USNA, 1910)
Was kind to his crew in 1941-42 while commanding the battleship New York (BB-34), 54-55; ran the ship aground in 1941, 55, 57

Weather
During World War II, the battleship New York (BB-34) sometimes escorted merchant ship convoys during dense fog, 63-64